# GOD our Loving Enemy

# GOD our Loving Enemy

## W. Robert McClelland

87-1689

ABINGDON
Nashville

GOD OUR LOVING ENEMY

*Copyright © 1982 by Abingdon*

**Library of Congress Cataloging in Publication Data**

McCLELLAND, W. ROBERT (WILLIAM ROBERT), 1931-
God our loving enemy.
1. God—Wrath. 2. Fear of God. 3. Christian life—Presbyterian
authors. 4. McClelland, W. Robert (William Robert), 1931-
5. Spastic dysphonia—Patients—Missouri—Biography. I. Title.
BT153.W7M37     231.7     81-12680     AACR2

**ISBN 0-687-15220-8**

Unless otherwise noted Scripture quotations are from the Revised Standard
Common Bible, copyrighted © 1973, and are used by permission.

MANUFACTURED BY THE PARTHENON PRESS AT
NASHVILLE, TENNESSEE, UNITED STATES OF AMERICA

To Dottie and the Hope Community of Faith
who never thought me diminished
in the days of darkness

# Contents

# Preface

In no sense is this book or its title meant to be irreverent, much less clever. On the contrary, I trust these pages exhibit the greatest reverence and respect for God—sometimes known as the fear of the Lord. Indeed, it is just this fear of God that seems to be missing from so much popular theology today which refers to God as if he were a cozy chum. It is in vogue to speak of God casually as if he were our best friend who has nothing better to do than smile upon us in a beatific manner endorsing our day dreams. Such language seems trite, if not vacuous, to those who have experienced God in bone-rattling encounters which can only leave them God-shy, yet awed by his Grace-Fullness. To speak of him as the Enemy at least does not undervalue such encounters and clears the air of pious, but empty language so we can be ripped open again to the awesome experience of meeting God face to face—and discovering Life.

Those who have never experienced God in this way will find these pages an enigma. I ask for your tolerance, if not understanding, of a religious experience different from your own. Those who have experienced life in this way will find here an invitation to identify the adversary as God and learn of his grace. Those who have felt guilty about their rage against God and have drifted away from the community of believers because the church did not understand their experience will find here a word of permission to own those feelings and discover again the People of God.

It is to some of those people that I must pay my dues because writing a book, like giving birth to new life, is never an isolated event nor a solitary enterprise. There are those who are responsible for the conception and others who help in the delivery. To Raleigh Wilson who first dared me to risk believing I had something to share, I am indebted. To Richard Kimerle, Joyce Williams, and Sue Trail, who encouraged me to put my sharing into writing; to Roland Tapp, who made me believe I could write and offered suggestions along the way, and also to Linda Spires who insisted that I write and spent arduous hours in deciphering my manuscript typing it into a legible form, I owe debts of gratitude. I am indebted also to Janet Mertz and Bonnie Montle for their help in proofreading the final results. Finally, I owe a debt of gratitude to you, the reader, who do me the favor of reading my work and in so doing, make all the effort worthwhile. Thank you.

W. Robert McClelland
*St. Louis*

# Introduction

By profession I am a minister and a theologian; by training, a public speaker. I make my living by talking about God. Ten years ago I lost my voice. My career seemed to be at an end, since the demand for preachers who cannot speak is less than minimal. I was without my voice for four and a half years. In retrospect, I see those years as an experience I would never choose to go through—if I had the choice to make—yet neither would I trade them, now, for anything. During that time I experienced the despair of hell and the wholeness of heaven. I found God to be the enemy, only to discover him to be the God of grace. The old wine skins of my traditional faith were split open by the new wine of my experience. In these pages I want to share with you how it happened and what I learned from my pilgrimage, believing that many of you may encounter God in a similar way.

During the late winter of 1972 I suffered a case of the flu which, in turn, brought on laryngitis. My speaking voice was reduced to a whisper. I always dreaded having a cold because invariably it would settle in my chest and end up as laryngitis. These periods of voice loss usually lasted a week, during which time I would reduce my speaking engagements as much as possible. Where it was impossible to rearrange or cancel, I would whisper into a microphone in order to be heard. Thus, I was not overly concerned when my voice was slow in returning. It was an inconvenience, but I could manage to cope with it.

However, when my voice did finally begin to come back, I noticed it was increasingly difficult to speak. Every sentence was an effort. It was as though the vocal cords, like a swinging door hanging on rusty hinges, were frozen into place. Every word—every syllable— had to be forced through them. Both the feeling and the sound was like trying to talk while strangling.

By spring I had been to several throat specialists who looked for the usual and the unusual: nodules on the vocal cords, tumors of the throat, obstruction of the windpipe. I was referred from one physician to another. Finally, a doctor diagnosed my problem. It was spastic dysphonia.

I had never heard of it before. I was told, matter of factly, that it was rather uncommon, tended to occur among "executive types," and was "incurable." The word burned itself into my consciousness. I was relieved to know that my condition had a name. To know that the mystery had been solved offered, momentarily, the prospect of hope—but then the word "incurable" came down like an iron curtain.

After the initial shock subsided I began to hear what else the doctor was saying about my disease. It could be arrested, he thought, with the aid of voice exercises.

In the next several weeks I began speech therapy, even as I checked with other doctors about spastic dysphonia and their view of the prognosis. They were agreed: it was not a common disease; the prospects for recovery were not bright; they were not clear on what causes it; and therefore assumed it was "psychosomatic." That was the second blow. Not only did I have an incurable disease, but its origins were suspect. To be labeled as one with psychosomatic illness was to be branded as one who did not have his head on straight, or so I thought. The doctors at the Mayo Clinic gloomily intoned that even with psychoanalysis the outcome could not be considered hopeful. Not only did I have an "incurable" disease, I concluded, but equally as bad, my head was on *hopelessly* crooked.

Increasingly, over the next several months I felt like an albatross had been hung around my neck. I felt ugly. I sounded ugly—therefore, I must *be* ugly. Since it was such an effort for me to speak I withdrew from small-talk conversations, saving my energy for my professional obligations: preaching, teaching, and counseling. Because I felt myself forced into an exile of silence, I felt as though people would think me dull—even stupid. My wife had to do most of the social talking for us both. More and more I felt like the wooden dummy dragged along because she did not know what else to do with me. My mind taunted me, "She thinks you are a dummy because you can't speak. Others have to talk for you." In point of fact my wife never once felt that way, nor did she accuse me of being antisocial. Never once did she make me feel conspicuous, unwanted, unrespected, or unloved. All these feelings were generated by my own deteriorating self-image. If spastic dysphonia was not psychosomatically caused before, it was fast becoming so.

Because speaking was such a difficult way of expressing myself, kicking the dog, slamming doors, and pounding on tables became the means of expressing my frustration. But frustration only leads to further frustration. It was important to identify the source of my frustration. I had to locate the enemy. As Job knew so well, it is God who stands behind our suffering. As Jesus found out, it is God who assigns us our crosses. Since, as a Christian, my faith was in God, he was the one on whom I vented my frustration. He became the target for my rage.

Gradually, I began to slip into a depression. Since my self-image and self-confidence had, from high school days, been built upon being able to "talk a good line," my affliction had dealt me a crippling blow. As an adolescent I had more than my share of not-OK feelings. I was not the athletic jock in high school or college. I was neither a lover nor a lady-killer. I had been able to put my act together on the basis of my humor, entertaining others with my gift of gab. My dues to the human race were paid by my ability to talk. In seminary I gained recognition—not for my academic achievements—but as a budding preacher. There I excelled, winning the preacher-of-the-year award. After my graduation and ordination I was installed in my first church, where I made a name for myself through preaching. It is an occupational hazard that we preachers fall in love with our voices and begin to develop a "ministerial tone." There are not many professions where people hang on every word you say. Your voice becomes of central importance. You make your living by speaking. Eventually you discover yourself expecting people to listen to you. It can be a heady brew. For me, it was intoxicating, and my ego became addicted to it. I needed to have people like me as a preacher.

But how could anyone like me as a preacher if I did not sound nice? How could anyone like me as a person if I could not talk? My identity as a preacher was in jeopardy, and my self-confidence as a person was being eroded. No church would want me as their minister I feared. Worse, my wife would no longer want me. Just as my self-worth as a minister diminished, so, too, did my self-worth as a marriage partner.

I thought of leaving the ministry and my wife. The thought of suicide crossed my mind several times. These at least seemed to be easy and attractive ways out of my misery. But not *that* attractive! Instead I sought counseling and began therapy. Over the next year I learned a great deal about myself, but there was no change in my voice. I tried hypnosis and biofeedback—all to no avail. Friends encouraged me to go to faith healers. I knew I was being prayed for, and several times hands were laid on me in healing attempts. If ever the gates of heaven were battered with the prayers of faith, it was for my healing and the recovery of my voice. But the gates of heaven remained closed, as did the swinging doors of my vocal cords. For four and a half years I strangled as I spoke.

There was no improvement in my voice. I carried on as usual, including my preaching and teaching responsibilities; occasionally accepting a speaking engagement outside of my own parish.

It was on these occasions that I was acutely reminded again of my voice problem because people would comment on it, ask questions about it, or sympathize with me concerning it. The people of my own congregation had long since dismissed it from their minds which, of course, made it possible for me to be less self-conscious about it. It is to their everlasting credit that it never occurred to them that a preacher who talked funny would not have something to say or be able to serve them.

Gradually, there appeared a change in me. I no longer thought of myself as a handicapped person. My congregation did not. Why should I? I no longer felt like a cripple. I came to accept myself—as I was—croaky voice and all. More importantly, I began to like who I was. If a psychosomatic illness was the price I had to pay for having risked living, then I would wear it proudly as a red badge of courage. Slowly I came to value myself as a person—a unique miracle of God's creativity. Gradually, I came to value myself as a preacher—not because I sounded fine—but because my experience had given me something to say. I found, within myself, a growing self-respect as a marriage partner who had something to offer the relationship, and as a human being who had gifts to share with others. For me, this was the most difficult hurdle of all. It meant risking belief in myself—daring to accept new stories about myself and letting go of the old ones. It meant an inversion of my old value system, a relocation of my identity as a preacher, and discovery of my worth as a person.

There are many factors that contributed to this metamorphosis. The counseling therapy was invaluable in helping me come to an understanding and acceptance of myself. But its effect would have been minimal if my family and the Community of Faith had not surrounded me with the amazing acceptance, support, and love that were the vehicles of God's Grace.

But there was another vehicle for that grace: the grappling with scripture in what became a dialogue about life in general and my life in particular. Because I am a minister, I had to say something about God and Christian faith every day during those four and a half years. Precisely because of my voice loss, the ensuing depression, and the eventual acceptance of myself as a miracle of God's creation, whatever I said had to square with my experience. If Christian faith had nothing to say to me, I had nothing to say to anyone else. My own depression put me in no mood to play games, and my difficulty in speaking left me with little energy for sharing superficial clichés. The gospel had to have a saving power from depression, a word of hope for the incurably ill, and make sense of my Joban encounter with God.

The problem was that traditional Christianity gave me very little help. It seemed to have no knowledge of my experience with God as the enemy. It called my way of speaking of God blasphemy at best and a total loss of faith at worst. Fortunately, in the pages of the Bible I discovered it was neither.

The usual theological understanding of the divine-human encounter is that God loves us, and we are, therefore, to adore him. As a result, Christian worship is customarily heavy with praise and thanksgiving.

Such an understanding of worship is, however, too narrow. It omits many of the moods and emotions that I and others feel in relationship to God. Such feelings are candidly displayed by the heroes of faith in the Bible. Consider Job, for example. Picture Job sitting on his dung heap, shaking his fist in the face of God, demanding that God respond to his demands for justice. For him to sing the Doxology seems inappropriate, if not ludicrous.

Jeremiah, the young prophet, delivered his message of doom and destruction day after day, only to be met by the laughing ridicule and scorn of his audience. In private, he laid his complaint before God and demanded that God shape up or allow him to ship out. Adoring silence would not be his style.

The Psalms are filled with cries of dereliction and anger, demanding revenge born of emotions other than adoration and praise. Have these moods no place in worship or in our relationship to God? How, then, did they get into the Bible?

Whatever else the Bible is, it is a book representing the varied experiences of the People of God. Those experiences are portrayed with the rich colors of deep emotions: rage, love, jealousy, repentance, pride, and stubbornness. It is unfortunate when the Bible is regarded as merely a collection of names, dates, and places. Its importance is even lost if we regard it as a collection of propositional statements about God, Christ, or sin. Behind the names, dates, and theological assertions of the Bible stand the experiences that give them their significance. When we see the Bible as a collection of stories and faith statements reflecting people's experiences with life, their ups and downs, their joys and sorrows, it comes alive with amazing wisdom and power. In and through these stories is reflected an experience of new humanity, which the Bible refers to as "being born again," "set free," "raised from the dead," "healed," and the like. It is this *experience* of deliverance from death to life which the Bible is concerned about sharing and from which we can benefit. In addition to whatever resources it has for those concerned about heaven, it offers us permission to join the human race, here and now.

This, therefore, is not a book about a preacher who lost his voice—poor fellow! It is rather a book about the God whom many of us encounter as the enemy and the biblical stories that serve as a faith resource in understanding the experience. It is, to use D. T. Niles' analogy, one beggar telling another beggar where to find food.

The value of scripture is that it represents an experience greater than our own. It interprets our individual story in light of the larger story told by the People of God as they encountered life. Their story enlarges our view of what relationship with God can mean beyond the traditional one and thereby makes room for large numbers of people—and their experience of God—who might otherwise be excluded. The insights to be found there can be of great value to us as we live out the days of our lives. To be sure, the Bible experience is couched in the thought pattern and world-view of a different age. However, its concern is not to convince us that the world is a three-storied universe but rather to share its understanding of what it means to be human. It is that understanding to which I want to bear witness.

# God Is a Heavyweight

And Jacob was left alone; and a man wrestled with him until the breaking of the day. When the man saw that he did not prevail against Jacob, he touched the hollow of his thigh; and Jacob's thigh was put out of joint as he wrestled with him. Then he said, "Let me go, for the day is breaking." But Jacob said, "I will not let you go, unless you bless me." And he said to him, "What is your name?" And he said, "Jacob." Then he said, "Your name shall no more be called Jacob, but Israel, for you have striven with God and with men, and have prevailed. . . ." And there he blessed him. So Jacob called the name of the place Peniel, saying, "For I have seen God face to face, and yet my life is preserved." The sun rose upon him as he passed Peniel, limping because of his thigh.

Genesis 32:24-31

What a curious story. Jacob wrestling with an angel of God. Hardly the stuff of which holy writ is made. Yet the story presents itself as the personification of Israel's relationship with God. As such, it represents the experience of a large number of people, greater, in fact, than Israel's population. Many of us have found our well-ordered lives invaded by the Divine Heavyweight,

*21*

and we have the wounds to prove it. It is, therefore, not only Israel's story; it is ours as well.

Old Testament interpreters have usually explained the story as Jacob wrestling with his guilty conscience for depriving Esau of his inheritance. But when we lay this struggle up against some of the other great wrestling matches of the Bible, such an interpretation does not hold up too well. Take, for example, Job. Job wrestled with the silence of God, demanding some word from the Lord which would justify his innocent suffering, calling God every name in the book because God would not answer him.

Jeremiah, one of the Old Testament prophets, wrestled with God because he had a word from the Lord that seemed ridiculous to the people and was embarrassing for him. People laughed and said, "Look, here comes Jeremiah. Let's hear what he has to say today, for it will certainly be entertaining. He prophesies doom, but business has never been better." Jeremiah shook his fist in the face of God and called him to account for the fact that nothing was happening. It is a classic example of the struggle between obedience and its consequences.

Out of the New Testament steps Paul whose conversion encounter with God on the road to Damascus ended up with him being thrown to the ground and blinded for several days. It would appear, therefore, that there is more to the curious story of Jacob and the angel than merely a guilty conscience. Rather it would seem the Bible assumes that struggle is a normal part of life and growth.

All the way through the Bible we find this theme played again and again. Genesis begins with the assumption that man shall earn his living by the sweat of his brow, struggling with the environment to make it productive. Children will be born only at the price of pain as woman struggles in labor to give birth to new life. In the book of Exodus we find that the Hebrews gained their freedom from Egyptian oppression and obtained a land to dwell in only at the price of conflict and bloodshed. Even the Twenty-Third Psalm, which is probably the most popular and reassuring of all the psalms, speaks of the table of life being spread in the presence of our enemies.

When we come to the New Testament we find the same theme. Jesus began his public ministry locked in a wrestling match with God over the meaning of his ministry. How was he to approach it? For forty days and nights he wrestled with the question. Indeed, he continued to struggle all through his career, as is clear in the Garden of Gethsemane, and in that cry of dereliction from the cross, "My God, my God, why?" From birth to death, the Bible seems to assume all of life is a struggle.

What is most surprising in the story, however, is the suggestion that it is God Himself who is our opponent. God is the one with whom we wrestle. He is the enemy. Israel was to discover that she was locked into a covenant relationship in which God had both promised and threatened to be her God and to make of her his people. In times of doubt and uncertainty, Israel found that promise reassuring and comforting. But in times of

23

emerging nationalism, she found the promise to be a threat standing tall in her path as she sought her own glory and self-aggrandizement. Nowhere did that promise become more of a threat than in the words of Amos, who, speaking on behalf of God, said to a wayward Israel, "You only have I known, Israel. You only have I pledged myself to. You only have I made these promises to. *Therefore*, I will sell you into bondage. If you fail to get the message the first time, then I will have to play rough with you. I will make of you my people, or I will break you. I have started something with you, and I intend to finish it" (paraphrase, Amos 3:2). There is a delightful scene in Edith Sommer's play, "Roomful of Roses" in which a little girl asks her mother if she has ever considered divorcing Daddy. The mother is shocked and insists, "No, never." Then the mother thinks for a moment and responds, "Murder, yes. But never divorce."[1]

That is the meaning of the covenant between God and Israel. It is as if he were saying, "Murder, yes, but never divorce. We will have to fight it out, Israel, because I have no intention of leaving you. But remember, *I am a heavyweight. And I will win.*"

So this story in Genesis of Jacob wrestling with the angel needs to be understood against the much larger background of Israel's whole relationship with God—a constant wrestling match in which God was shaping and molding Israel in spite of, or because of, her wishes in the matter. The point of the story is uncomfortably clear. Life is one big wrestling match, and our opponent is none other than God.

But if struggle is a normal part of human existence, why then do we try to avoid it so?

Certainly none of us in our right mind enjoys conflict. The person who meets life with a chip on his shoulder and enjoys fighting with everything and everybody is sick. There is something wrong with a person who enjoys arguing over the back fence with his neighbors instead of talking with them. Indeed, Jesus made it very clear, peacemakers wear the white hats. Most of us avoid conflict because we have been taught that it is un-Christian. Conflict is to be avoided at all costs because there is something alien about it to the Christian life.

But the story of Jacob's fight with the messenger of God is not about bickering with our neighbors. It is speaking of a wounding encounter with life which, in fact, is the encounter with God. Our desire, therefore, to avoid such conflict may be born of fear or at least laziness. We do not like being interrupted. When we get our act put together, we do not like someone unraveling it. We do not like changing our minds once we have made them up. Once we have worked out the answers to life's meaning, we want to close the books and go out to play. We do not want to be challenged in our beliefs. We do not want to consider other possibilities because those possibilities make us rethink our conclusions, and we become fearful when our position is not as secure as we had assumed.

Something very interesting happened in a class on contemporary theology I once taught. We were talking about Rudolf Bultmann, whom some people see as a threat to traditional Christianity because he challenges such ideas as the Virgin Birth, the Resurrection, and all the miracles. About halfway through the lecture, I noticed that the class had stopped taking notes. Not because they could not understand Bultmann's position, but because Bultmann's assertions were too threatening to be considered any longer. He was challenging some cherished ideas; and the intellectual wrestling match that he was inviting my students to enter was too threatening and therefore had to be avoided.

It is this kind of escape that is cut off by the biblical assertion that all of life is a struggle. It is no less than God who bids us enter into this wrestling match with him. Of course, that is threatening! Somebody could get hurt in that kind of a struggle. And because God plays for keeps and weighs more than we do, it is probable that we are the ones who will suffer the pains of growth. We are the ones who will suffer the wounds of change. After all, Jacob left the encounter limping.

As a result of our laziness or fear to enter into this kind of encounter with God there is within the Christian faith a subtle tendency to see God as a tranquilizer and to portray Jesus as his spokesman who says reassuringly, "Peace I leave with you. My peace I give to you" (John 14:27). There have been many who have seen this tendency as a heresy, but no one saw it more clearly than Karl Marx. As a result, he labeled religion the opiate of the people.

To be sure, the church has come a long way since the time of Karl Marx; but most of us would rather have

Christ portrayed in our churches and homes as the shepherd of the sheep, holding cuddly lambs in his arms and speaking soft, soothing words than as the disturber of the peace who says, *"I have not come to bring peace, but a sword!"* (Matthew 10:34), or, with the veins standing out on his neck, drove the money changers out of the temple shouting, "Robbers, get out of here" (paraphrase, John 2:16).

And lest we come to the conclusion, prematurely, that this was an isolated incident in his life, look at Jesus' whole relationship to the evil of his time as personified in the demonology of the New Testament. Take his healing ministry, for example. When Jesus healed a person there was a struggle. So vicious was the struggle that it was often described as "convulsing" the person, "throwing him down" on the ground so that he "appeared to be dead." When Jesus bade a man be healed, he bade him wrestle with the demons within him.

The same is true of the Resurrection. Before there could be a Resurrection, there had to be a Crucifixion. From the church's perspective the Crucifixion was the ultimate struggle between evil and God. Before the bonds of sin and death were broken, Christ had to enter into a wrestling match with the power of evil so titanic that the outcome was uncertain for three days.

Thus, when Jesus says, "Take up your cross and come follow me" (paraphrase, Matt. 16:24), his words need to be seen as something more than mere rhetoric. It is an invitation to a way of life. It is an understanding of how life really is to be lived. It is to be lived with

27

struggle. And the struggle is born of our adversary, God.

When Jesus said, "Peace I leave with you. My peace I give to you," he added the very cryptic words, "(but) not as the world gives." The world expects peace to be the absence of conflict. Peace as the world understands it, is the avoidance of struggle. The world calls this calm, peace. The Bible calls it an illusion. It is a figment of the world's imagination. The peace that Christ gives us is not what the world understands as peace at all, and therefore the world cannot offer it. The world sees people in conflict with themselves or with society as neurotic personalities, troubled people, or trouble-makers. They are not content with the status quo.

But the Bible does not view conflict as alien to life. Indeed, it sees it as very much a part of life. Struggle is not only normal, it is meaningful, because in it we are shaped by God. An old Chinese proverb speaks of crisis as a dangerous opportunity. Dangerous, because such crises never leave us as they found us. But from the perspective of this story, they can be seen as opportunities or occasions by which God forges our humanity on the anvil of struggle. God's image is hammered out in us when we take our lumps in the wrestling match with him.

We have little choice over the hand that life deals us, but we do have a choice as to how we will play it. Jesus offers us one possibility. When he says, "Peace I leave with you. *My peace* I give to you, (but) not as the world gives," he is saying "my peace" is not the absence of conflict or struggle. "My peace" is rather the realization that struggle is born of God. Therefore we can relax in the struggle. In playing our hand we can be assured that neither life nor death, nor angels nor principalities, nor things past nor things to come can ever separate us from God because the conflict is born of God, the heavyweight.

To put it more positively, as Paul did, "In everything God [the heavyweight] works for good with those who love him, who are called according to his purpose" (Romans 8:28). And that, says Jesus, is the peace which the world cannot give; for the world does not understand peace in that way.

Consider the picture of a ship resting quietly at anchor in a harbor. The water is calm. The sun warm. A peaceful scene, the world would say. But notice the ship is going nowhere. The crew is lazily sleeping on the decks, and the cargo is rotting in the hold.

Consider by contrast the picture of a ship under full sail, heeling over hard in a stiff breeze, pounding through rough seas. Not so peaceful by the world's definition, but each crew member knows that the harder the wind blows, the faster the ship goes, and the sooner they will reach their destination. With the sting of salt spray in their faces, the crew is confident that the captain of the ship, a veteran of many years before the mast, knows what he is doing and is in full control.

That is the peace Jesus was talking about, and it comes from knowing that the God who stands behind life's struggle is a heavyweight who has our growth in mind.

# Run for Your Life

O Lord, thou hast searched me and known me!
Thou knowest when I sit down and when I rise up;
   thou discernest my thoughts from afar.
Thou searchest out my path and my lying down,
   and art acquainted with all my ways.
Even before a word is on my tongue,
   lo, O Lord, thou knowest it altogether.
Thou dost beset me behind and before,
   and layest thy hand upon me.
Such knowledge is too wonderful for me;
   it is high, I cannot attain it.

Whither shall I go from thy Spirit?
Or whither shall I flee from thy presence?
If I ascend to heaven, thou art there!
If I make my bed in Sheol, thou art there!
If I take the wings of the morning
   and dwell in the uttermost parts of the sea,
   even there thy hand shall lead me,
   and thy right hand shall hold me.
If I say, "Let only darkness cover me,
   and the light about me be night,"
   even the darkness is not dark to thee,

the night is bright as the day;
for darkness is as light with thee.

Psalm 139:1-12

One of the characteristics of the Bible that continues to commend it to our reading is its ability to hold a mirror to our lives. This psalm is a good case in point. Unfortunately, the usual interpretation fails to do so, with the result that the point is missed. The church has generally assumed that the psalm tells us something about God. Thus we are to take these words as a theological statement that tells us of God's ability to know everything and to be everywhere present. The God with whom we have to do business has a perfect knowledge of us, all our thoughts and actions are naked and open before him. This, of course, is a very orthodox interpretation. It is also very dull. What else would you expect of God? So what else is new?

However, if we look at the psalmist's words not so much as a theological statement, but as an autobiographical statement, the perspective is radically altered. This second way of interpreting the psalm tells us about the psalmist, not about God. God is not spoken of in some abstract way, but as the result of a personal encounter. On the basis of his experience, the psalmist is telling us what it is like to meet the reality of God.

Now the plot begins to thicken, and we are led to ask the question What kind of experience would produce such a description? Old Testament scholars agree that this psalm is an enigma. It is not like anything else in the book of Psalms. It is not a psalm of joy. We instead

*31*

sense a kind of panic, as if the psalmist were running for his life and cannot get away. Nor is it a psalm of lament. There is not a note of sorrow in it. It certainly is not a thanksgiving. It is written more like a complaint. The psalmist complains to God that he has no privacy whatsoever. If he goes to the left or to the right, God meets him. He does not even have the privacy of his own thoughts. God already knows them. He is beset behind and before. He cannot go up and he cannot go down. God is to be found everywhere.

Normally God's presence with us brings a sense of security. The good news is that God is always in touch with us and will not desert us. If we are trying to find peace of mind by holding on to God's coattails and are afraid that if we ever let go all will be lost, it comes as a blessed relief to hear that we no longer have to live in dread. God has hold of our coattails. God will not let us go. Ours is a God of loyal love. He will not forsake us. He has promised to be our God and has assured us that we are to be his people. We are, therefore, free to risk living. These are tidings of great joy.

But that kind of love can be frightening. It is precisely that terrifying aspect of God's love about which the psalmist is speaking. He cannot get away from God.

One of the interesting phenomena in the Bible is the response of fear that comes over people when God confronts them. Look, for example, at the sixth chapter of Isaiah where he describes his vision of God. His response is, "Woe is me. For I am lost; for I am a man of unclean lips, and I dwell in the midst of a people of unclean lips" (Isaiah 6:5).

Remember Luke's Christmas story? A band of angels appeared in the night sky to announce the arrival of the Messiah. But the reaction of the shepherds was such that an angel had to reassure them, "Be not afraid; for behold, I bring you good news of a great joy" (Luke 2:10).

Or consider the experience of Jonah, who had other things on his mind than preaching, trying to flee in a boat from God's call to him. Jonah was terrified as he was tossed about in a storm and was finally thrown overboard. He was stalked by a great fish and then swallowed alive, kicking and sputtering. All because God's love, that terrifying, stalking love, would not let go of Jonah even though he wanted to vacation in the sun on the French Riviera and attempted to run away.

The hymn, "O Love That Will Not Let Me Go," takes on a strangely different meaning when it is heard on the lips of Jonah. Or on the lips of Francis Thompson, who in the poem "The Hound of Heaven," describes God's relentless stalking of him:

> I fled Him, down the nights and down the days;
> I fled Him, down the arches of the years;
> I fled Him, down the labyrinthine ways
> Of my own mind; and in the mist of tears
> I hid from Him, and under running laughter.
> Up vistaed hopes I sped;
>     and shot, precipitated,
> Adown titanic glooms of chasmed fears.

And finally when God's love backed him into a corner from which there was no escape, Thompson declares:

> Naked I await Thy love's uplifted stroke!
> My harness piece by piece,
> Thou has hewn from me,
> And smitten me to my knee;
> I am defenseless utterly.
> I slept, methinks, and woke,
> And, slowly gazing, find me stripped in sleep.

Love of God? Yes. But a loyal love that will not let go. A terrifying love that will not give up. It is this threatening love that has gripped the psalmist. God will not leave him alone. There is no place to go to get away.

> Whither shall I flee from thy Spirit, O God?
> Where can I go? If I ascend up into heaven,
> Thou art there. If I make my bed in
> hell, thou art there. If I seek to
> escape into sleep, calling darkness
> around me, it lights up and I cannot
> sleep. Thou art there. If I go to
> the fore or the rear, Thou art there.
> If I think at all, Thou art there.[1]

The psalmist is trapped. This is why his poem is an enigma. It is not a psalm of joy, praising God. It is not a psalm of thanksgiving. It is not a lament. In despair the psalmist is complaining, "O God, where can I go to get away from you?" And the irony of it is that he cannot go anywhere. Neither up nor down, forward nor back. He cannot escape his despair. The God who normally brings comfort and alleviates despair is precisely the God who has brought the psalmist to the verge of panic. The psalmist utters his words in a cold sweat. He has met the Enemy.

What are we to say about this? Is the psalmist some kind of nut? Is this some kind of perverted experience of God alien to our understanding of the faith? Perhaps. But it is not alien to the biblical understanding of the faith. Nor is it alien to Christ's understanding of how God meets us. "I have not come to bring peace, but a sword," says Jesus (Matthew 10:34).

Too often we have interpreted that sword as having to do with social justice, which indeed it often does, as it cuts through the hypocrisy of the church's lack of attention to the injustices within society. But I think the real meaning of Jesus' words becomes clear if we set them against those other words of his, "Peace I leave with you. My peace I give to you, [but] not as the world gives" (John 14:27).

We are, by nature, anxious creatures. Life conspires to make us insecure. Doubts assail our faith from within, and uncertainties bombard us from without. Our health fails, our business goes down the drain, loved ones disappoint us. Death constantly stalks our life, reminding us of our end. The specter of meaninglessness hangs over our entire existence.

Instinctively we reach out and clutch life and loved ones to our bosom. All of us want to be secure. We all want peace of mind. But by peace we mean an absence of anxiety, and the only way to get rid of anxiety is by holding at arm's length all the threatening circumstances, all the unsettling questions, all the doubts, all the deaths of life. So, we party a lot, or talk about the

35

weather, or take a trip for our health in an attempt to flee from our anxieties. We even cover our dead with cosmetics so the reality of death does not have to be considered.

When doubts overwhelm us and disturb our tranquility, we sometimes draw rigid boundaries around our beliefs. We defend those boundaries with fanatical zeal, lest our faith falter. Doubt is too unsettling to be entertained as a house guest.

We cover up our failures in life with rationalizations designed to explain just why things did not come off the way they were supposed to. Rationalizations are intended to protect us from the intrusive gazes of others and their comments about our failures.

The problem is that we never quite pull it off. Peace and security are elusive. We do not find them. Any peace or security we have is always undercut, sooner or later, by the other doubts and threats which constantly stalk our being. Our loved ones die and leave us alone. Our messiahs fail us. Our causes are seen to be tarnished. The harder we try to nail life down, the more devastating is our failure. Certainty is a myth. Peace and security are not part of this life. Our cities crumble, our beliefs change. Our bodies grow old. Sooner or later we have to come to terms with the fact that we are vulnerable. Our lives hang by a heartbeat, and eventually we must do business with death—our death.

The hush that comes over us in a funeral parlor is not so much born of our respect for the dead as it is of our awareness that sooner or later this is where we, too, will be. It is this feeling, therefore, of devastating failure to find security and peace that the psalmist and Jesus were talking about. This feeling of despair looms large when we see that there is nowhere in life we can go to escape our anxiety, neither to the Riviera for a vacation nor out for another drink. There is nowhere we can finally rest secure and say, "I am safe!"

What is most amazing, however, is the psalmist says that God meets us in our despair. When we know that we cannot escape anxiety, when we know that we cannot escape insecurity, when we know that worry and imperfection are part of the human scene, we meet God—the disturber of our contentment, the invader of our lives—God: the enemy. When we know that we cannot escape by sleeping or taking an aspirin, by going out on the town or entering a monastery, jogging to keep in shape or dyeing our hair to hide the gray—in short, when we are on the verge of panic and have come face to face with despair, peace comes. The peace of God—the peace which passes all human understanding. The peace which this world cannot give, just as Jesus said.

I can remember the peace that came over me when I finally accepted the fact that my voice was not ever going to get better. After having gone from doctor to doctor, after having tried this remedy and that therapy, after having followed all the well-meaning, but fruitless, advice of friends, I finally faced up to the fact that I was never going to talk easily again. I finally was able to say to myself, "This croaky old voice is going to be my means of speaking for the rest of my life." Then, and only then, when I could no longer escape, did I relax and get on with the job of living.

It is precisely when we know we cannot escape, when we know we cannot win in the struggle against the aim and the end of our being, when we see that the despair which hounds and haunts us is more powerful than our ability to resist—at that point, says our psalmist friend, we see the face of God. For despair is another name for God. We realize that the one who haunts us until we face up to ourselves, our limitations, our imperfections, and our end; the one who hounds is no less than God.

Therein lies our hope because there is no way we can escape God. All the hounding is born of that terrible love that will not let us go or let us settle for less than himself. Our security rests not in insurance policies or in theological answers to threatening questions, not in rationalizations which excuse us or in looking both ways before we cross the street—our security rests in no less than God.

Paul Tillich, in speaking of this experience, says:

Grace strikes us when we are in great pain and restlessness. It strikes us when we walk through the dark valley of a meaningless and empty life. It strikes us when we feel that our separation is deeper than usual, because we have violated another life, a life which we loved, or from which we were estranged. It strikes us when our disgust for our own being, our indifference, our weakness, our hostility, and our lack of direction and composure has become intolerable to us. It strikes us when, year after year, the longed-for perfection of life does not appear, when the old compulsions reign within us as they have for decades, when despair destroys all joy and all courage. Sometimes at that moment a wave of light breaks into our darkness, and it is as though a voice were saying: "You are accepted. *YOU ARE ACCEPTED*, accepted by that which is greater than you, and the name of which you do not know.[2]

The name is often called despair because we meet it at the point where we know we can no longer escape. It is at the point of despair that we encounter the grace of God. For when we make our bed in hell, behold, he is there.

It is only then, as we look back at the events that brought us into despair, that we see the loving hand of God. We might not choose of our own volition to go through those events ever again. But in the midst of them we know that we cannot escape. We run for our life, but our adversary has blocked our escape. We find that we are beset behind and before. God has laid his hand upon us. We are trapped. It is because he will not let us go that we are reduced to the despair that is the peace of God. We know we are in the hands of God. The God who will not let us go. The God who has called us to life and growth.

# Grace Is Not the Name
# of a Girl

In the last chapter we spoke of God as despair. Since all of us know something of despair, all of us know something of God. Our problem is that often we do not recognize him with whom we are dealing. We meet him in those experiences when our lives are uprooted and our plans are demolished, but we are reluctant to admit that our adversary is God. It is, however, important that we name him properly. Only when we correctly identify God as the enemy can real relationship with him be possible. I would refer you to the experiences of Job as well as the psalmists, who found that authentic communication with God began, not on the mountaintops of inspiration and celebration, but in the depths of suffering and despair. "Out of the depths I cry to thee, O Lord!" (Psalm 130:1). Paul Tillich goes even further and argues that if we have never met God as the enemy, we have never met God at all.

It is safe to say that a man who has never tried to flee God has never experienced the God Who is really God. When I speak of God, I do not refer to the many gods of our own making, the gods with whom we can live rather comfortably. For there is no reason to flee a god who is the perfect picture of everything that is good in man. Why try to escape from such a far-removed ideal? And there is no reason to flee from a god who is simply the universe, or the laws of nature, or the course of history. Why try to escape from a reality of which we are a part? There is no reason to flee from a god who is nothing more than a benevolent father, a father who guarantees our immortality and final happiness. Why try to escape from someone who serves us so well? No, those are not pictures of God, but rather of man, trying to make God in his own image and for his own comfort. They are the products of man's imagination and wishful thinking, justly denied by every honest atheist. A god whom we can easily bear, a god from whom we do not have to hide, a god whom we do not hate in moments, a god whose destruction we never desire, is not God at all, and has no reality.[1]

Martin Luther was terribly shocked when he recognized the hatred of God that existed in his own heart. All of us harbor that kind of hatred, but we are very successful in masking it. All of us have a quarrel with God, but most of us vent our venom by quarreling with others. I am sometimes upset, for example, with my wife when other responsibilities call her away from home. I am upset with her, but I am really fighting the aloneness of life. I get angry with my children and kick at the dog when they do not see things as I do and fit into my well-ordered plans for existence. But I am really rebelling against the oncoming death that has no interest in my plans and disrupts my existence. I want to nail life down and hold onto the good times, but I cannot, and I resent not being able to do so.

Part of the beauty of Job's story is its candor and honesty. Job is not afraid to air his dirty linen in public. There is no phony fighting with his wife. There is no hypocritical kicking of the dog. Job shakes his fist in the face of God, the author of his life, the author of his aloneness, the author of his suffering, and the author of his death, and he says, "*Why,* O you my enemy?!"

God meets us in our happiness and says, "It shall pass." God meets us in our youth and says, "You will grow old and feeble." God meets us in our enthusiasm and says, "The world will not respond." God meets us in our anxiety and says, "That's life!" God meets us in our reaching for crutches and pulls them away. God meets us in our search for meaning and demonstrates its absurdity. God meets us in the midst of life and pronounces death. The God of Job is the God of the Crucifixion.

But the God of the Crucifixion is the God of our Lord Jesus Christ who gives us permission to call him, "Our Father." I will be quite honest with you. If it were not for Jesus Christ, I would find it difficult to believe that God really cares. But Jesus calls God "good," and in my book he is credible. Jesus went to his death thinking that his dying would serve God.

It would be one thing to go to our death with the bands playing and the banners flying, taking a stand with everyone in the gallery applauding. But it is something else to go through what Christ did, knowing that we had to do it absolutely alone. One by one, the props were stripped away from Jesus. First, Judas went out to betray him. Then Peter denied him. Christ's mission faded before his eyes. One by one, the disciples fell away until Jesus was left alone hanging on the cross, his ministry ending in disaster. When it seemed as though even God had deserted him, he cried out, "My God, my God, why have you forsaken me?" (paraphrase, Mark 15:34). The whole universe held its breath with that question. He could have denounced the fickleness of the crowd or the weakness of the disciples. He could have said, "To hell with the whole bit. Nobody cares. Why should I?" But he hung there. His last words were, "It is finished" (John 19:30).

I want to suggest that in this mucked-up world there is one thing that is absolutely dependable and that is Jesus' trustworthiness. His credibility is beyond reproach. When all of a man's supports are stripped away, including his God, and he is left standing there utterly alone—faithful to the end—*there* is a man who can be trusted. Jesus Christ is credible. And it is Christ who says, "You can call God good. You can call him loving Father." Despite all the evidence to the contrary, Christ gives us permission to call God good.

That is the absurdity of the faith, which, as Christians, we profess. We believe God is a Father who cares. And like a caring parent, who is willing to endure the anger and hatred of an adolescent son or daughter because he wants him or her to grow and mature, God encounters us in our adolescence, enduring our anger and rebellion, because he cares and wants us to grow and mature. He wants us to live in the world of *reality*.

Most of us have a rather adolescent attitude about suffering. We assume that suffering and human trauma are bad things that should be avoided, or better, removed at all costs. This is especially true for us as Christians living in America, where suffering and death are incompatible with our dream of vigor and success. Our faith in medical technology has caused us to see pain as a no-no and death as a defeat. Hence, we have devalued the experience of suffering. In our denial of pain we have denied our encounter with reality; we have little to say to suffering people, preferring instead to hide them from view in nursing homes or confine them to ghettos. As people who enjoy a high standard of living and the benefits of a comfort technology, we see suffering as foreign and out of the ordinary, instead of seeing it as the common experience of all people, and especially of all people of faith. Whatever else we may say about the crucifixion, it is a constant and threatening reminder that suffering and trauma are inescapable—even for the Son of God! Thomas Kelly reminds us:

> If you will accept as normal life only what you can understand, then you will try only to expel the dull, dead weight of Destiny, of inevitable suffering which is a part of normal life, and never come to terms with it or fit your soul to the collar and bear the burden of *your* suffering which must be borne by you, or enter into the divine education and drastic discipline of sorrow, or rise radiant in the sacrament of pain.[2]

That same adolescence expresses itself in our demands for justice in life. How many times as a parent I have heard my children say, "That isn't fair. I won't do that. I have my rights!" Like Job in his adolescence, we come before God and demand justice. "Why me? Why should I suffer? What have I done that is so grotesquely evil as to deserve all this?" We forget that nowhere and at no time has the Bible promised us fairness in life, much less a rose garden flourishing in the soil of justice. "Why not me?" is perhaps the more appropriate question.

Job comes to God with a preconceived idea of the way life is—or ought to be. He assumes this is a moral universe in which morality is defined by good guys winning and bad guys losing. Because he is good, he ought not suffer. So he lays his complaint before God, whom he imagines, wears a white hat and demands justice. But God responds in silence! Chapter after chapter God turns the other way because he is not interested in Job's preconception of the way things *ought* to be. No reasons are offered to Job because God wants to bring Job into a new reality. He wants to escort Job into the world of his presence.

The real world is not ordered by Job's preconception of the way he thinks it ought to be. The new reality is that life contains mystery and absurdity. Job discovers life is not reducible to his understanding or comprehension. Indeed, God comes to Job as the enemy destroying his adolescent *idol of justice* in order that Job can come to know him as the *God of Grace*.

Grace is not the name of a girl. It is the name of the

45

God who encounters Job as his enemy. It is the name of the God who gives him life without reasons—who gives him the miraculous opportunity of living without justifying that opportunity to him or without his having earned it. Grace is the miracle of life given him with all the joys and sorrows that come with it, yet without any more of an explanation of the one than the other.

By the end of his story, Job understands who his enemy is: the God of grace. He therefore no longer regards his existence, his possessions, his lot in life, as being the result of his deserving. He sees his life rather as a gift of grace, given with no explanation attached, a gift which is as much of a mystery as is his suffering. He understands neither why he should suffer nor why he should have been called to live at all. Both are mysteries. He now lives not by answers but by amazement.

Grace is our life, given to us. Thornton Wilder, in *The Eighth Day*, puts it this way: "When God loves a creature He wants that creature to know the highest happiness and the deepest misery—then he can die. He wants him to know all that being alive can bring. That is His best gift."[3]

God's best gift is to know all that being alive brings. It is as if God were saying, "You might never have been, but you are! And now that you are, I want you to experience all that being alive means. I want you to feel joy and sorrow; I want you to experience laughing and crying; I don't want you to leave here without knowing what this amazing gift of life is. I want you to look around you! It is for you that I created this universe, and I love you. I offer you all of the resources of my being: my strength, my joy, my endurance, my wisdom, my peace, for your living. All of these I offer you, but I do not give you reasons. I have called your life into being, and I want you to be amazed, and there is no room for reasons in amazement." That is the meaning of grace.

Had it not been for the Resurrection, we would never have thought about the Crucifixion a second time. We would have assumed, with the Stoic or the Cynic, that crucifixions and suffering are just the human lot. So we are to tough them out. But the Resurrection story will not let us settle the matter so easily nor so fatalistically. The Resurrection makes us look again at the Crucifixion. It reveals that suffering and death are a part of God's will for human life. They are part of life's goodness. There are no reasons to justify that assertion. No reasons are offered to make sense of it. The story of the Resurrection simply affirms that the Crucifixion is OK by God, and thereby we are given permission to pick up the pieces of our lives and begin to live them again. Faith in the Resurrection is the most radically creative response that we can make to life. The question still remains, Why suffering? and no answer is given by the Resurrection. Certainly the usual answer that suffering is God's punishment is not affirmed. But the Resurrection does affirm life with its suffering as good life. It affirms life with all its joys and sorrows as a gift of God's grace.

Perhaps the closest we can come to a reason for suffering is that when life is pleasant we do not need to live by faith. Everything makes sense. When life is good, our relationship with God can be, and often is, superficial. Our prayers are often no more than pious words, a tip of our hat to God. But when life tumbles in, when the bottom drops out, and we stand with Job and the psalmists in the pit of despair, then we are doing business with a reality that we cannot escape. Our relationship takes on an intensity and an urgency not present before. That is why for the psalmist and Job, and for us, authentic communication with the God of grace does not begin until we have encountered Him as the Enemy.

> Out of the depths I cry to thee, O Lord!
> Lord, hear my voice.

# In Defense of Rage

Encountering God as the enemy may cause us to cry out in anguish or reach out in rage. Both are genuine responses to God's invasion of our lives. Both responses can be found in the psalms. Since the psalms of Israel were originally sung in temple worship, some of them are roughly the equivalent of swearing set to music. Take, for example, Psalm 22:1-4

> My God, my God, why hast thou forsaken me?
> Why art thou so far from helping me, from
>     the words of my groaning?
>
> O my God, I cry by day, but thou dost
>     not answer;
> and by night but find no rest.
>
> Yet thou art holy,
> enthroned on the praises
> of Israel.
> In thee our fathers trusted;
> they trusted, and thou didst deliver them.

or Psalm 139:19-22

O that thou wouldst slay the wicked, O God,
and that men of blood would depart from me,
men who maliciously defy thee,
   who lift themselves up against thee for evil!
Do I not hate them that hate thee, O Lord?
   And do I not loathe them that rise up against thee?
I hate them with perfect hatred;
   I count them my enemies.

By sad contrast, I doubt if, today, you can find a hymn that expresses rage. You will find hymns of adoration and praise, confidence and faith; hymns having to do with calmness and peace, commitment and loyalty. But no hymns at all having to do with anger and rage. No swearing set to music.

That would seem to suggest that there is no place in the church for enraged people. Apparently the church knows little of God the enemy, or else there is a massive conspiracy of silence about such knowledge. It has provided little in the way of theological handles for understanding him as our adversary. As a result, many left alone with their feelings of anger against God, drift to peripheral edges of the church and are condemned to live with guilt. Worse, they think they have lost their faith. The church says, as my mother used to say, "You mustn't be angry. Certainly, not with God." Indeed, religion looks upon anger as wicked, and rage against God as blasphemous. As a result, many of us go to church only to come home and slam the door, bitch at our mates, or harp at the kids.

Yet strangely enough, we ignore Christ's anger. More likely, we excuse it. When Jesus chased the money changers from the temple, we call it righteous indignation. We have baptized his rage with a new name and thus made it all right for Jesus to feel that way. But not us! Such feelings are not permissible, not even among the biblical models of faith. Thus we label Job as patient. Job was anything but patient, shaking his fist in the face of God, demanding that God justify his torment and suffering. Traditionally, we leave out those verses in the psalms that exhibit rage, pretending they are not there, no doubt hoping that if we ignore them they will go away. The question is, however, If anger has no place in the Christian's life or in the life of the community of faith—what do we make of such examples of faith as these in the Bible?

I want to suggest that these models of rage are in the Bible precisely because the Christian faith assumes that rage is a normal part of our encounter with life, which is simply another way of saying that rage is the normal part of our encounter with God. Two of the most important words in the Old Testament are "listen" and "speak." The relationship between God and his people is a dialogic relationship of listening and speaking, of praising and complaining, arguing and singing.

That is the nature of Job's relationship with God. Job sits on his dung heap, complaining to God and accusing him to his face, "You have done me dirt. My well-laid plans for an ordered life have gone down the drain. The expected justice of the universe that I had counted on is gone. The meaning of life I now see to be a figment of my imagination. God, what in heaven's name are you doing?"

The collapse of meaning happens to all of us periodically. Some months ago our household was stunned by the tragic plane crash that killed Congressman Jerry Litton and his family. Although I never met the man personally, it was like a death in our family. I suppose we identified with the Littons through our son, Steve, who was intimately involved in Litton's senatorial campaign. Through his eyes, we came to know Jerry Litton as a man of integrity, warmth, and energy. After the polls closed that Tuesday night and the returns came in, Litton's upset victory became apparent. Steve called us long distance to share his joy. Then came news of the tragedy—the entire family killed in a plane crash on their way to the victory celebration.

We talked often on the phone that week, my son and I. Once the initial shock settled into the numbing reality of the tragedy, Steve's response was as predictable as it was normal. He was angry with God. The absurdity of it. The utter futility of it all. The utter waste. The total nonsense. His faith was shaken, and he called God every name imaginable. He shook his fist in the face of God, saying, "My God, my God, why . . . ?"

For me, the experience opened an old wound. Several years ago when I was on the faculty of a midwestern college, I sat by the hospital bed of a colleague's wife. Night after night I prayed her to sleep as she fought a losing battle with diabetes and a malfunctioning kidney. Shortly before Christmas I was called to the hospital because the doctor said she was not expected to live through the night. I prayed by her bedside and mobilized the community of faith among the college students and faculty to pray for her healing. We had gathered and prayed daily and diligently. Now we battered the gates of heaven with our prayers. A miracle occurred. The crisis passed. Within a few days she was well enough to go home and spend Christmas Day with her family. God was good and gracious. It was reassuring to know that he agreed with our reasoning. Obviously, he was healing our friend. After all, did it not make sense to heal her? Her husband was just coming into the faith, and she had two young children who desperately needed her. What a marvelous display of God's power this was. In the midst of the agnostic, academic community this was tangible evidence that God was alive and well, and that faith made sense. So we celebrated the miracle of Christmas Day. But that night, when the celebration was over, she took a turn for the worse and had to be taken back to the hospital. New Year's Day she died.

I was asked to have the memorial service. But I vowed to God that I would not make any excuses for him. "This is your doing, God," I accused. "You get yourself off the hook. I'm not going to be your public relations man. If you've got any good news, you tell them. This was your idea, not mine. If this is what you call wisdom, you explain it!"

The memory of my raging against God came back as I talked to Steve and listened to him curse God in the face of the mute tragedy. Like father, like son.

The books of Job and the Psalms offer some great models of what being human means in the face of God.

When we do not rage in such a world and with such a God, we are holding out on him. Like a woman who talks to her psychiatrist instead of her husband, or a man who pounds out his frustrations in the workshop instead of complaining to his wife, we are holding out on God and cheating in the relationship. When we stand before God, there are times when rage is the only appropriate response. Unfortunately, our church liturgies never give us the opportunity to express it. Most prayers are a coverup. The psalmist reminds us we must have no stonewalling at the altar.

"But why do you blame God?" someone is probably asking. "It was a disease that took your friend. It was carburetor icing or mechanical failure that caused the Litton plane to crash. Why don't you blame them instead of God?"

I submit that it is terribly important to identify the enemy correctly, and the enemy is God! How can you rage against a piece of metal such as a carburetor? How can you rage against a kidney? How do you work through those emotions of absurdity with a carburetor or a kidney? No! God is the one to be blamed.

One of the major assumptions of our faith is that the meaning of being human is to be in relationship with God and with our fellow human beings. Hence, Jesus summarizes the law by saying, "Love God, and love your neighbor" (paraphrase, Luke 10:26, 27). As most of us know, to pretend as though everything is sweetness and light in a marriage, when, in fact, there is something galling one of the partners, is not only to shut down communication, but to play a hypocritical game in which true relationship can never develop. The same is true of our relationship with God. To pray to God with unclenched fist when our emotions are boiling and demanding some kind of response from God who seems to be out to lunch is both hypocritical and, in the last analysis, destructive to our whole relationship with him. The point is simply that the Christian faith gives us permission to be angry with God when we sense, as we often do, God's indifference to our dreams, our hopes, and our ambitions.

After all, it is God who has sentenced us to death. Not to feel some anguish or sense of outrage at the extinguishing of the miracle that is our life, is, I submit, not really to understand either the miracle of life, on the one hand, or the finality of death, on the other.

An officer of the French Foreign Legion once said to his men: "You Legionnaires are soldiers in order to die, and I am sending you where you can die." Some of us have felt that way about God. He created us for threescore and ten years, or even if by reason of strength, fourscore years, yet those years are soon gone, and they pass away like a sigh. It is as if God were saying to us, "I am creating you to die, and I am putting you where you will die."

Sitting atop one of the mesas in New Mexico a few months ago, I contemplated the miracle of erosion that had carved the landscape; water and wind wearing away the rock, leaving those towers of rock stretching for miles and reaching thousands of feet into the air. It took millions of years to etch such beauty. And there I was counting my threescore and ten years, saying,

"God what's the hurry? Why are you so impatient with us when you have such infinite patience with the rest of your creation?" Woody Allen once quipped, "I don't want to achieve immortality through my work; I want to achieve immortality by not dying." His humor unmasks the real issue for us. In a more sober moment Allen gets right to the heart of the matter when he says:

> It's very important to realize that we're up against an evil, insidious, hostile universe, a hostile force. It'll make you ill and age you, and kill you. And there's somebody—or something—out there who, for some irrational, unexplainable reason, is killing us. [1]

It is important to know who our enemy is because if the Enemy is not identified correctly, we inevitably blame the wrong person; we fight with our spouse or shout at the children.

Look at those marvelous models of blasphemy in the Bible: Job, Jeremiah, the psalmists, even Jesus. They knew who the Enemy was. They knew with whom they were doing business. "My God, my God, why have you forsaken me?" You do not say, "Shh, shh, don't say that," or "It isn't God's fault . . . God is nice." When we are enraged at God, cursing God becomes the expression of the relationship. That is why Karl Barth says, "Blasphemy . . . , even the blasphemy of Job, is blasphemy against God," not emptiness. [2] Cursing God is as much an affirmation of faith in God for the person who hurts as is singing the Doxology for the person who is happy. The difference in style is where life finds us.

The real problem arises when, in the raging, we say

that God is dead. The temptation is to say, "We will have nothing to do with you, God. If that's the way you are, we're finished. You're dead—or might as well be."

Richard Rubenstein, the Jewish theologian, contends that after Auschwitz it is impossible to believe in God any longer. The theologian concluded a paper that he was reading before a symposium with the statement that God is dead. The next speaker laid aside his prepared speech and spoke extemporaneously. His name was Elie Wiesel. Wiesel, also a Jewish theologian and writer, is a survivor of Auschwitz. Rubenstein is not. Wiesel said, "How strange that the philosophy of denying God came not from survivors. Those who came out with the so-called God is dead theology, not one of them had been in Auschwitz. Those who had [been in Auschwitz] never said it."[3] To be left living in a world without God is no problem—it just does not make sense. That is not a hard choice, explains Wiesel. "No! If you want difficulties, choose to live with God. Can you compare, today, the tragedy of the believer to that of the non-believer? The real tragedy, the real drama is that of the believer." To deny God, to say that he is dead, immediately eliminates the problem. But to be a believer is to be condemned to the struggle. "My God, my God, why . . . ?" For the believer, human experience raises the question of God's character.

In one of his books, Wiesel writes with imagination of what it might have been like for Adam, the first human being, to open his eyes and find himself alone in the world. Wiesel suggests that in our aloneness, the elementally human question is not "Who am I?" but

"God, who are you?"[4] From the beginning it has always been a question of God's character, not his reality.

It makes sense to curse God. But it makes absolutely no sense to deny him, because we cannot run far enough away to escape the tragedies that haunt us and call into question the meaning of life and the goodness of God. It makes as much sense to deny God as it does to deny life, for God is Life. So the first thing we have to say about rage is that the Bible, through its very models of faith, gives us permission to be enraged at times with God when we see him as our enemy.

But not everybody becomes angry. Not everybody is enraged with either God or life. If my mother were living, she would not understand this chapter at all. I can identify with Dylan Thomas's words, referring to the onslaught of death, "Do not go gentle into that good night. / Rage, rage against the dying of that light." But there are many people who cannot. Death is for them a normal, natural process. It is taken in stride by faith. So the second thing we must say about rage is that not everybody has been given the gift of rage, yes, *gift*.

If anger is to be seen as something other than a sign of immaturity or a symptom of a deep-seated neurosis, then it is important that within the community of faith we call it a gift, a gift of God.

I assume all of us are neurotic. We differ only by a matter of degree. But I want to affirm that our very neuroses are the creative means developed by our psyches that enable us to survive life's onslaught and adapt to it. Neuroses can be seen, therefore, as God's protective gifts to us. Our neuroses are the creative means by which God not only enables us to survive, but etches into our personality the uniqueness that gives us something special to offer to life and to others. We could say, for example, of the Old Testament Prophets—those angry men and women who came down out of the hills to protest the injustices of society—they had trouble with authority figures. Or we could say they just could not adjust to the status quo; they had trouble fitting in to the norms of society. But the fact of the matter is that they could not have been prophets without that particular neurosis. Without the gift of rage, they would simply have gone to church with the masses and never have seen or been disturbed by the wrongs about which they spoke. An associate of newspaper columnist Jack Anderson once said that the dominant characteristic of all investigative reporters is their sense of outrage. One simply will not be a good investigative reporter without it. Interestingly, and perhaps appropriately, the organization that brings together investigative reporters and editors is called IRE. In any case, let us look at rage as a gift from God.

To see rage as a gift of God carries with it the responsibility of investing our gift responsibly in his service. Rage that goes no farther than mere blasphemy soon becomes cynical. To curse God and die, as Job's wife suggested, is the tragic waste of a gift. Ernest Hemingway could not stand the fact that he could not control life and live it on his terms, so in a fit of rage, he committed suicide. What a senseless waste! A much better way is to direct our rage—not against ourselves nor against life—but against God. Francois Mauriac tells of Elie Wiesel's rage against God in the concentration camp.

> On the last day of the Jewish Year, [he] was present at the solemn ceremony of Rosh Hashana. He heard thousands of (his fellow) slaves cry with one voice: "Blessed be the name of the Eternal." Not so long before, he too, would have prostrated himself, and with such adoration, such awe, such love! But on this day he did not kneel. The human creature, outraged and humiliated beyond all that heart and spirit can conceive of, defied a divinity who was blind and deaf. "That day, I had ceased to plead. I was no longer capable of lamentation. On the contrary, I felt very strong. I was the accuser, and God the accused. My eyes were open and I was alone—terribly alone in a world without God and without man. Without love or mercy . . ."5

We accuse God in order to show him what love is. We accuse God in order to show him what mercy looks like. When we have had it up to our eyeballs with the indifference of life and the deafness and blindness of God, there is one thing left to do with our rage and that is to accuse God by our *actions*, by our loving actions, by our merciful actions, bringing into the absurdity of this life some humanity.

Again, Woody Allen's humor is on target, "If it turns out that there is a God, I don't think he is evil. I think the worst thing you can say about him is that he is an underachiever."6 Allen's humor offers a very penetrating look at life. Anyone with eyes and sensitivity can see the underachievement of God in this world. We see the social injustices. We see human frailty and the absurdity of undeserved suffering. It is this rage at God's underachievement that motivates us to act and to show God up. A faith without rage accepts things as they are. A faith without rage expects that merely praying will take care of everything, and we have no further responsibility for shaping history. That can be a colossal copout. That is why Wiesel speaks of the silence of God as God. The deafness of God is God, the blindness of God is God. Only then, when we are enraged, do we take responsibility for our world and act to show God and the world what love and justice look like. To be fully human in a world of injustices is to be given to rage. People who cannot feel rage never become radically involved. They may write their congressman or pass out leaflets, but they cannot throw their whole weight against the inertia of history.

On December 4, 1955, Rosa Parks got on a bus in Montgomery, Alabama. She had worked hard all day and was tired. When she was told to stand and move to the back of the bus, she refused because she was not only physically tired, she was morally tired, tired of the injustices of segregation. That quiet act of outrage was the beginning of the civil rights movement. Martin Luther King, Jr., provided the charisma needed to focus the energy of blacks, but he could not have done it without the underlying volcano of moral outrage among them.

Several years ago a remarkable transformation took place in an East Los Angeles community of slum housing, high crime, and neighborhood deterioration. The Chicano residents began to paint murals on the sides of the buildings. Amazingly, the crime rate began to decline. People began to take an interest in their neighborhood. Not because it was beautiful art, but because, as the Mexican muralist, José Clemente Orozco said, "Murals are a screaming public message." The residents had expressed their rage in their murals and were again able to feel a sense of integrity that, in turn, enabled them to take pride in their neighborhood. When we are able to scream out, in our rage, who we are, we come to feel a certain sense of worth. We are again able to become responsible citizens in an outrageous world.

So we find that Christian faith gives us permission to be enraged. But it dares us to see rage as a gift and calls us to invest that gift like all gifts—to the glory of God.

# Growing in Faith

The time is fulfilled, and the kingdom of God is at hand; repent, and believe in the gospel.

Mark 1:15

Mark sets Jesus' call to faith in the context of wild beasts, the wilderness, and the arrest of John the Baptist. Such a context reminds us that when Jesus calls us to repent and believe the good news, he speaks to us as those who know loneliness, suffering, and death. It is in such a context that we are called upon to repent and believe.

The ability to repent and believe is a growing process. Despite the spectacular nature of some sudden conversions, the development of mature faith takes times. The apostle Paul is a case in point. Though he experienced a sudden conversion on the road to Damascus, he spent considerable time alone in meditation before beginning his preaching ministry. One of the characteristics, therefore, which distinguishes Christians is their growth in faith.

When we speak of growing in faith, however, most of us think in terms of becoming a better person:

increasing our capacity for patience and kindness, growth in gentleness, expanding our understanding of what it means to be a disciple of Christ. No doubt my wife might think my growth in patience and understanding is desirable. My friends might want me to enlarge my capacity for love and concern. I assume most of us want to become better persons.

But the New Testament makes it plain that God is not concerned with our becoming bigger, better people. He is not impressed by our goodness or by our growing ability to be patient, kind, and loving with one another. Paul, with one swipe, levels all our attempts to become better people by saying, "None is righteous, no, not one" (Romans 3:10).

God does not measure the relative difference between us regarding our ability to love. He gives no points for being more generous and less arrogant than another. Indeed, as if to underline the point, Jesus says that the tax collectors and the prostitutes will get into the Kingdom ahead of the church-going, Bible-reading, praying people. To rub salt into the wound, Jesus interprets the law so that it is impossible to comply with it. "You know the law: You shall not kill. But what that means, friends, is that anyone who is even angry with his neighbor has already broken the law. You have heard it said, 'You shall not commit adultery,' but what God had in mind is that everyone who has ever lusted after another person has already committed adultery in their heart" (paraphrase, Matthew 5:21-22, 27-28). The bottom line of New Testament concern is to make sure that we understand, once and for all, that there is nothing we can do that will impress God, nor cause the doors of his Kingdom to open for us as if we had earned the right to enter. Until we understand that premise we can never understand the biblical claim concerning the miracle of God's acceptance of us as we are. The good news presents us with the amazing permission of God to live our lives as vulnerable, flawed human beings or, as Paul Tillich puts it, to accept the fact that we have been accepted.

Our eagerness to grow in faith, therefore, stems from the mistaken understanding that growing means expanding our present abilities, adding to what we already have, enlarging what we already know. Therein lies our mistake, for Christ calls us to grow in faith. He is not talking about growing in goodness or enlarging our understanding. He is talking about growing in faith, faith in God, the God whose name is despair and who meets us as the enemy. The God whose wisdom appears to us to be foolish, and whose strength appears to us as weakness and whose love seems to be opposition. We should have had some inkling that we were heading down the wrong path when we heard Jesus' call to repent and believe. Jesus is not calling for repentance from moral failure. He is not saying, "Knock off your sinfulness." Rather, he says, "Repent and believe." The two go together. "Stop and have faith. Turn around—you are growing in the wrong direction. You cannot add to what you already have, for you have nothing. You cannot enlarge your understanding, because you understand nothing. Repent and believe. Grow in faith."

We must now raise the question, In what are we asked to believe? In what are we asked to have faith? The answer is disturbingly simple. We are asked to believe in the Cross. *We are asked to have faith in death*—our death. We are invited to believe that the scandal of our dying is not an obscene insult to our integrity, but the ultimate gift of God to us.

The Cross is God's sentence of death. Across all our activities lies the shadow of the Cross. Death is the *no* that God speaks to all of our plans and efforts. It is the *no* that is written across all our hopes and ambitions.

Consider Jesus as a teacher; the record has it that he was a very creative and popular one. If he were on a university faculty, he would have published extensively and been an authority in his field. Students would seek him out and be influenced by his wisdom. He would have tenure and could look forward to a long and useful career as a wise man. But no! God's will for him was "the foolishness of the cross."

Jesus was a healer. The Great Physician, he has been called. He could have been chief of staff at any large hospital. Everyone he touched was healed, made whole, brought back to life. Yet every person he healed eventually died. God's answer to them and to his promising career was *no*! Eventual death was the outcome of all his healing activity.

Jesus was a wonder worker. Think of the entertaining tricks he could perform. He could have held an audience in the palm of his hand, spellbound, and gotten them to do anything he wanted. As a most sought-after celebrity, he would have been able to draw people magnetically to him and then tell them the good news of God's love. But God's response to this appealing prospect was "No! I have in mind for you the scandal of a cross." The New Testament is agreed on at least one point: God's will for Jesus was death.

The Cross stands at the boundary line between human striving and God's will. Death is the line of demarcation between our control of life and God's. It marks the divide between belief in ourselves and our dreams; and faith in God who has his own plans for us. The Cross is the last frontier. It is where all things human cease, and God alone reigns supreme. Karl Barth puts it succinctly, "The last day of man is the first day of God." When we are left finally at that boundary line, only one thing can be said, "My God, my God! Why?" At that point we stand on the brink of faith in God. It is at that point where there is nothing more to know, nothing more to say, nothing more to be done, nothing except the one important thing in life and that is to have faith; that our task is to trust God and assume that he cares and is caring, that the Enemy is really our Father.

Faith stands on the other side of the Cross, not on this side. Each of the disciples, this side of the Cross, followed Jesus for selfish reasons. Each of them had his own agenda. James and John wanted to sit in the place of honor in the kingdom of God, one at the right of Jesus, the other at the left. They wanted God to fit into their plans. Judas betrayed Jesus only when it became evident that his own intentions would not be carried out, and he would not be a powerful person in a worldly kingdom. The farthest thing from Peter's mind was a crucified Messiah. "God forbid, Lord! This will never happen to you" (paraphrase, Matthew 16:22), he assured Jesus. We confidently assume that we know what is best for us and what it is that we need to grow in our faith. But for us to decide what we need to grow in our faith is to insure that we will never take on anything too risky, anything really beyond our convenience, anything irrational or too uncomfortable. If we were the architects of our spiritual growth we would forever remain in shanty town because our plans are inevitably quite different than God's plans. We have great things in mind such as power, fame, and success, or at the very least, peace of mind, happiness, and security. God says to grow in faith is to believe in death—our death.

It is only at the human extremities that we finally "let go and let God." As long as we have any strength at all, we try to control our life, shape it according to our definitions and understanding. Recall the story of the soldier who, during the war, was afraid for his life and prayed, "O God, I haven't bothered you for twenty years, and if you will just help me through this, I won't bother you again for another twenty years." He is typical of us all. So long as we have any control over our life at all, we want to manage it. We want to be in charge. It is only at the extremities of life that we call upon God. It is only when everything else fails that we let go and let God.

Death, symbolized by the Cross, represents the final letting-go of our life. It is the final acknowledgment that life is not at our beck and call, and never has been; that we are not in control, and never will be. To grow in faith is, as Jesus says, to stop and believe the good news; believe in the Cross, have faith in death. Death is God's best and most loving gift to us, for it teaches the ultimate lesson about relationship with him. It reminds us that we are designed to live by faith in him. Sooner or later we will understand that fact of our nature. Death insures the learning.

Such a lesson cuts deeply into our naive assertions that we are in control. It shatters the myth that we are, or can be, self-made individuals. Such myths are nourished by our society's success cults and are the little darlings of the positive—or possibility—thinkers among us. But Christian faith has always resisted long association with such wishful thinking and has correctly seen such ideologies as heresies. Christian faith speaks of faith in God—not in ourselves. It calls us to repent and believe, not merely to affirm our ambitions.

If we are to believe in death as God's good gift to us, then dying is the only way we can grow in our faith. There are no shortcuts to the Resurrection. There is no way around the Cross. In a variety of ways God reminds us of this fact by pulling the rug out from under us, inch by inch. The two-year-old who encounters the no of her parents is reminded that the world does not revolve around her desires. The forty-year-old man who faces the fact of growing older, futilely tries to fend off the aging process by staying in shape or dyeing his hair. The idealist who wants the world to measure up to his expectations is disillusioned by God as the injustice of the established system prevails. The child, innocent and pure, discovers the contingency of life when she happens upon an accident in which someone has been killed. The marriage partner who, after fifty long years of sharing life together, finds in the death of the beloved that, in the last analysis, only God is dependable. All of us faced with our threescore and ten years, sooner or later come to realize that "our years come to an end like a sigh" (Psalm 90:9). No wonder the psalmist says, "The fear of the Lord is the beginning of wisdom" (Psalm 111:10). Thomas Kelly's statement is classic.

> It is an overwhelming experience to fall into the hands of the living God, to be invaded to the depths of one's being by His presence, to be, without warning wholly uprooted from all earth-born securities and assurances, and to be blown by a tempest of unbelievable power which leaves one whole proud self utterly, utterly defenseless, until one cries, "All thy waves and thy billows have gone over me" (Ps. 42:7).[1]

In a hundred subtle and not so subtle ways the Enemy dismantles our illusions about reality, because he is calling us to grow in faith and believe in the wisdom of death. Soren Kierkegaard put it:

> The bird on the branch, the lily in the meadow, the stag in the forest, the fish in the sea, and countless joyful people sing: God is love! But under all of these sopranos, as it were, a *sustained* bass part, sounds the *de profundis* of the sacrificed: God is love.[2]

Growth in faith is developing our ability to sing the bass note of the sacrificed, "God is love." It is the note sung by those of us who cry out, "Why me?"—those who say, "Not now, Lord," or "Let this cup pass from me." We cry out, "My God, my God! Why?" It is to such as we that Jesus says repent and believe the good news. To have faith is to turn away from the conclusion demanded by the evidence, namely that life is absurd; and in turning away, to sing with all the condemned the bass note, the *de profundis,* "God is love."

The only way we can grow in that faith is by dying. Can we trust him with our death? I do not know. Can we be sure? Certainly not. We are talking about faith, not certainty. We are talking about trust, not knowledge. But we can try out faith. We can test that kind of trust by risking it in the little deaths we experience everyday. Life's little deaths become the practice fields for faith. As we practice our faith, we can be coached by, and draw assurances from, the stories of those who have gone before us—those who call back over their shoulders that the God who appears to be the enemy and who calls us to the Cross is, in fact, the God of grace.

# Crucifixions Have God's Approval

It is time now that we look directly at the Crucifixion. There can be little doubt that the passion and death of Christ have captured the imagination of the church and stand at the center of its faith. The Gospels spend more time dealing with the events of the last week of Jesus' life than all the rest of his life put together. The Christian faith has wrestled with the meaning and significance of the Crucifixion for twenty centuries. It is the focal point for theological discussion and debate. The Cross is the one and only universal symbol of Christianity. It is found in all churches, everywhere. It stands at the very center of our faith. We forget it only on pain of losing our identity as Christians.

Yet the Cross is perhaps the greatest embarrassment and most perplexing mystery of our faith. What philosophy, what psychology, what sociology can make sense of it? But there it is at the center of our consideration. Not the gold or silver cross of church altars or fashion design, but the cross of ingenious torture and public ridicule. We must do business with a rough, splintery cross. And we must conduct our business from this side of the Resurrection. Whatever we may say about it, we must view the Cross through the lens of the Resurrection.

Peter's first sermon recorded in the Acts of the Apostles takes up the issue and raises the question, "What is the meaning of the Crucifixion in light of the Resurrection?"

> Men of Israel, hear these words: Jesus of Nazareth, a man attested to you by God with mighty works and wonders and signs which God did through him in your midst, as you yourselves know—this Jesus, delivered up according to the definite plan and foreknowledge of God, you crucified and killed by the hands of lawless men. But God raised him up, having loosed the pangs of death, because it was not possible for him to be held by it.
>
> (2:22-24)

Peter's sermon commends itself to us not only because of its brevity—a virtue not often found in sermons today—but because it attempts to come to grips with the meaning of the Cross as he views it from the perspective of the Resurrection. We will examine Peter's words in due time, but first let us look at how the church has sought to answer his question.

Liberal theology has seen the Crucifixion as the confrontation between the demonic and dehumanizing forces of life and the power of God. The Resurrection, therefore, is seen as God's decisive and powerful action in breaking the back of the opposition and establishing his kingdom among people. The Resurrection assures us that God reigns. It acclaims that Christ has broken the back of the rebellious resistance. Christ has freed

73

the world from the power of evil. Christ has made of this world his kingdom. Harvey Cox in *The Secular City* uses the analogy of a revolutionary power taking over a country: though we may yet wait for the victorious new regime to appear publicly on the balcony, we know that the victory has been secured.[1]

Unfortunately, the evening news and the life experiences of countless numbers argue otherwise. There seems to be precious little evidence to substantiate such an optimistic view. How can we take seriously the assertion that Christ has secured the victory when millions of people go to bed hungry at night and thousands of people die each day of starvation? How can we say that Christ is victorious in a world where we live with wars and rumors of war? To say that Christ has won the war makes little sense to vast portions of the world's population. They know that the resurrection of Christ, whatever else it may have done, has not overcome life's crucifixions. The answer offered by such a theology is dismissed as so much Pollyanna gobbledygook.

Orthodox theology avoided the conflicting evidence of the news headlines by placing the implication of the Resurrection beyond this world. Christ's victory over sin and death, it said, has to do with life after death. Sin and death reign in this world, but Christ has provided a life in heaven free of both sin and death. The Resurrection provides a doorway into such a life. *Someday*, but not now, we will enjoy life everlasting with God in heaven. *Somewhere*, but not here, we will live where sorrow and sighing will be no more.

This, indeed, is good news for many people. Anyone who has ever walked in the valley of the shadow of death or has been with those who have had to make such a pilgrimage, know the power of Christ's words: "I am the resurrection and the life; he who believes in me, though he die, yet shall he live, and whoever lives and believes in me shall never die" (John 11:25-26).

But for many others, those words hold no meaning—not yet, at least. Heaven may be their home, but they are not homesick. They have no interest in another world beyond this one. If the good news of the Christian faith cannot address itself to this life, here and now, it has no word to speak worth listening to.

What is interesting is that both liberal and orthodox theology view the Resurrection as the eradication of the Cross. The Resurrection in both is claimed as God's overcoming the Cross. No enemy here. God opposes crucifixions. The Resurrection is seen as the denial of the permanency or reality of crucifixions. It is the proof that God will not tolerate them. There is no place for such in his will. God simply will not allow them either in this world or in the next.

Peter's attempt to deal with the Cross stands in bold contrast to this view. When asked, "What is the good news?" Peter did not reply that the Resurrection was the victory over the Crucifixion, as if the Crucifixion were God's enemy. "Jesus was crucified by the definite plan and foreknowledge of God." Peter could only have said that from the vantage point of the Resurrection. If Peter had been asked, on either Friday or Saturday, "What is the good news?" Peter would have laughed—no, he would have cursed. "What a stupid question? There is no good news! God has nothing to say to us in our despair. God is dead. We are left in our distress." To those who live with the reality of the Crucifixion, he could only have said: "They are terrible things. Not only because of the pain they bring, but because they are graphic reminders that God is helpless and in hiding."

But the Resurrection changed all of that. As a result of it, the Crucifixion was set in a different light. The entire perspective was changed. The events of Friday and Saturday were the same. The Crucifixion was still a fact of history, nothing was undone. Yet the Sunday perspective made everything look different. Peter could say, "Jesus was crucified by the *definite plan and foreknowledge of God.*" On Sunday when he was asked, "What is the good news?" Peter replied that the Resurrection was proof that the Crucifixion had God's approval.

Notice, first of all, that Peter was not attempting to prove God or his relevance to nonbelievers—that would have called for a different approach. Peter was addressing himself to those who believed in God and who had been badly shaken by witnessing the crucifixion of Jesus.

Notice, too, that Peter was speaking as one who had gone through his own crucifixion. Not only had he been devastated by his unthinkable denial of his Lord and friend; he had seen his dreams for a messianic Kingdom go down the tubes with the death of Jesus. He was not a person who was unscathed by life's onslaught. He was no longer naively optimistic about his own abilities or the possibilities open to him in life. He had experienced the humiliation of failure, the coldness of fear, and the emptiness of doubt. He knew, firsthand, the weaknesses of human nature. He was aware of the vulnerability of human life which the Cross represents.

Peter, like Job before him, and many since him, had to make some sense out of his belief in God, on the one hand, and the reality of life's crucifixions, on the other. To believe in God and to experience crucifixion is to be forced to move toward either a belief in a God who is able to include crucifixions in his will or toward a god who is powerless against them. The one is larger than our ability to comprehend; the other too small to matter.

When we find ourselves looking at life from a cross the only question is What are we to make of our situation?

The faith experience of many blacks is instructive in this regard for they have had more than their share of crucifixions. Mrs. Fannie Chaney, interviewed by *Ebony Magazine*, had one son lynched in a voter registration drive in Mississippi in the summer of 1964 and another son killed in the Attica prison riot. She was asked how she managed to survive the two greatest storms of her life. Mrs. Chaney said of the God without whom there would be no life at all: "Whatever is going to be done, it will be His will. It may hurt, it may almost kill you, but the Lord will do His will. God's will must be done. I always try to lean on that philosophy."[1]

Neither Mrs. Chaney nor Peter is writing a textbook

on systematic theology. Their personal experience cannot be generalized or abstracted into theological dogma open to debate. They are not interested in creating or defending a doctrine of predestination. They are, however, vitally concerned with making sense of their belief in God and life's crucifixions. Without a God who is bigger than life's crosses, life would make no sense at all. Chaos would descend.

It is possible, of course, for us to affirm the absurdity of life and assume that there is no meaning in anything. But nihilism is not a possibility for those who are seriously wrestling with the biblical God. We must make some sense out of life because it is the glove on God's hand. As the psalmist says, "Thy hands have made and fashioned me; give me understanding that I may learn thy commandments" (Psalm 119:73). To cry out in anguish, therefore, "Why me? What have I done to deserve this? Must I drink this cup?" is to utter a confession of faith in God; the God of Job, Jesus, and Peter. The God who nails us to life's crosses. The enemy God who the Bible claims is the God of grace.

Like Job and Peter, Mrs. Chaney knows the love of God from personal experience. She also knows the reality of crucifixions. She either lives in a world where crucifixions are a part of God's will, or in a world of crucifixions where God is not relevant. Unless one has some assurance that crucifixions have God's approval, life makes little sense and chaos threatens. Such an understanding of the good news is not born of optimism. It arises because the Crucifixion is looked at from the perspective of the Resurrection.

We may ask, "Why would a loving God approve of a crucifixion—Christ's or that of anyone else?" Any attempt to give an answer to this question is, at best, awkward and clumsy. But it is a legitimate question and, therefore, deserves an honest response.

Crucifixions seem to be the means by which God changes us from one being into another. Jesus, for example, was changed from one who was bound by time and space to one who is free of all the limitations of this world. Similarly, Peter was changed from an impetuous boy, torn by doubts and fears, into a rock, worthy of a martyr's death, and upon whom the church could be built. This process of change is called growth.

Consider the experience of another black mother, Mrs. Paul Love, whose teen-age daughter was shot from a passing car while she was standing on a street corner.

> Since she's been gone, I done found out that I ain't frightened by anything. Not anymore . . . For instance, I'm not afraid to speak up anymore. I'm not afraid to speak my mind about how it is here in Mississippi. And I'm not afraid to die . . . And I done found out that I'm not afraid of airplanes any more . . . after Joetha died, I flew once to New York and then to Washington, and I figured then that if *she* could die the way she did, then I shouldn't be afraid to die the way I might.[2]

Mrs. Love, too, has found that through her crucifixion she has become a new person. She is no longer afraid of dying.

The Resurrection not only assures us that life's

79

crucifixions have God's approval, but because they have God's approval, we can be sure that the crucifixions cannot destroy us. They are, in fact, the occasions of growth, the doorways through which we pass into new being.

That fact, of course, may not be immediately apparent; at least not while we are hanging on our cross. But Peter's experience invites those of us who must carry a cross to risk assuming that our ordeal has not gone unnoticed by God and that, indeed, it bears his grace-full stamp of approval.

The good news of the Christian faith is that the Friday of crucifixion can be called *Good* Friday. That is the miracle. The good news is not only that we can find God in the joyous experiences of life and the blessings of health. Anyone can affirm such a God. Such a response is not really a statement of faith at all. The good news is that in addition to all these obvious tokens of his goodness, life's crucifixions are as much a part of God's grace-full will as the sunshine. That response *is* a statement of faith! Such a faith is made possible by virtue of the resurrection story. To those who believe in God and who know something of life's crucifixions, the good news is: crucifixions have God's approval. They are the means by which we grow. They are the means by which we are called into new creation.

# Humanity Approved

The new creation that God has in mind for each of us is called to life in a place called Bethlehem. Our familiarity with the oft-told story of Bethlehem sometimes fails to see the undesirability of the location.

In those days a decree went out from Caesar Augustus that all the world should be enrolled. This was the first enrollment when Quirinius was governor of Syria. And all went to be enrolled, each to his own city. And Joseph also went up from Galilee, from the city of Nazareth, to Judea, to the city of David, which is called Bethlehem, because he was out of the house and lineage of David, to be enrolled with Mary, his betrothed, who was with child. And while they were there, the time came for her to be delivered. And she gave birth to her first-born son and wrapped him in swaddling cloths, and laid him in a manger, because there was no place for them in the inn.

Luke 2:1-7

In *those* days—those days of Roman rule and oppression, those days of high taxation and hard times, those days when government corruption and the high cost of living were on everyone's mind as they conversed in the marketplace. Those days when Jewish zealots (that is, terrorists) were plotting the overthrow of the government and hijacking caravans. Those days when life was cheap and public executions—crucifixion-style—were hardly noticed. In those days—when the lame and the blind had resigned themselves to their careers of begging, like blind Bartimaeus sitting beside the dusty road going up from Jericho to Jerusalem, when tax collectors like Matthew and Zacchaeus had long since learned that the way to get ahead was to play the game and had willingly sold their souls in order to make a living. In those days—when prostitutes like Mary Magdalene, women of the city, had come to the cynical conclusion that the only thing any man would ever be interested in was their bodies. In those days, a decree went out from Caesar Augustus that all the world should be enrolled and taxed and taxed and taxed.

And all went to be enrolled. Dulled with resignation, weary to the bone, Joseph and Mary, tax collectors and prostitutes, all went to be enrolled in those days, plodding along the dusty, monotonous, wearisome road to Bethelehem. Bethlehem, the symbol of Roman oppression. The focus of financial hardship. The place where they were to be enrolled and taxed. The epitome of everything that was wrong with life—*Bethlehem!*

Every person has a Bethlehem. It may be the housewife who finds homemaking a dull and monotonous task with her college degree in a male-dominated society. Or the person who is told to report to the boss's office and makes the long, lonely trek down the hall knowing what awaits him behind the door. Everyone has a Bethlehem.

It may be the tyranny of the past, molded by expectations laid on by a compulsive world which confine and define us. We become what people expect, a self-fulfilling prophecy. They think we are shy, and we become shy. They think we are ineffective, and we become ineffective. They think we are worthless, and we become worthless. Everyone has a Bethlehem.

In his autobiography, Carl Jung describes his father, who had graduated from seminary and entered the ministry.

> His days of glory had ended with his final examination. Thereafter he forgot his linguistic talent. As a country parson he lapsed into a sort of sentimental idealism and into reminiscences of his golden student days, continued to smoke a long student's pipe, and discovered that his marriage was not all he had imagined it to be. He did a great deal of good—far too much—and as a result was usually irritable.[1]

Jung, in describing his father, paints a picture with which many of us can identify. "We live lives of quiet desperation," said Thoreau. Life is not all we had hoped it would be. Vexed and perplexed, pressed and oppressed, we plod along the dusty road to an appointment with our destiny and fate. We go to Bethlehem. Bethlehem is that place in the world where Jesus says we will have tribulation. Whether it be oppression or depression, boredom or hardship, all of us know something of what it means to live in Bethlehem.

Now it is precisely at this point that the miracle is seen. It is when we have stated the matter thusly that we are able to hear the good news. The claim our faith makes is that it was in *Bethlehem* in *those* days, in such a place, that Christ was born, the new creation established. It was precisely in Bethlehem that new possibilities and hopes broke forth, that history was invaded by novelty that surprised the cynics. There the potency of new actions erupted, the tyranny of the past was broken, and the terror of the future gave way to a new time. The dull destiny of the beggar Bartimaeus, the sellout of Matthew and Zacchaeus, and the cynicism of Mary Magdalene were forever altered and broken open in Bethlehem. The miracle of our faith is that Bethlehem is not remembered as a symbol of oppression, it is not remembered as the focus of financial hardship, it is no longer remembered as the epitome of all that is wrong with life. The miracle is that Bethlehem is remembered with joy because it was in that city, in those days, that the God of grace broke into the world with something new: new life, new beginnings, new creation.

This is the same miracle that transforms the Cross and the Crucifixion. The instrument of torture and death is remembered as a joyous symbol. It is remembered as an empty cross. It is a reminder that death is not Lord and that it need not define us or determine us. We may not be able to state the terms and the length of our existence, but the good news is neither does death.

By all odds, both Bethlehem and Calvary should be places that we would avoid. They are places undesirable, if not dangerous, to our health and happiness. But as Christians we keep returning to them at Christmas and Easter with great joy and celebration. Behind the stories of Bethlehem and Calvary lie the same grace-full experience. God's *modus operandi* is not to eradicate sin and death but to play "one-ups-manship" with them. He trumps their hand. Both Bethlehem and Calvary and the stories surrounding them remind us of the central miracle to which the New Testament bears witness. God meets us in the midst of real life with all its seaminess and sadness and uses both to create the new creature in us. This experience of creation and re-creation runs all through the Bible, but finds its clearest focus in the stories of Jesus' resurrection.

It is the reality of the resurrection experience which lies at the heart of the New Testament. The New Testament was written out of the immediacy of the Resurrection, and all its content is colored by the glow of Easter. Unfortunately, we were not there to witnesss the event, and we are left with difficult questions. How are we to interpret their accounts about it? What meaning does the resurrection of Christ have for us?

That we make something of it is absolutely crucial. Left as it stands, we have the story of a man Jesus, who was born and who died. Somehow he was resuscitated and came back to life. These details taken at face value make him a medical freak but hardly our Lord and

Savior. Until we begin to make some interpretation of the resurrection story it has no significance whatsoever for our lives. The Resurrection may be a curiosity, but it is hardly good news—not for us at least.

The most common interpretation of the Resurrection is to see it as the guarantee of eternal life, the proof that there is life after death.

The Resurrection thus becomes an example of what happens to us after death. But if this is our understanding, we cannot argue, as some have tried to do, that there is something significant or unique in Christ's resurrection. It is a matter of historical record that a belief in resurrection was already widespread by the time of Jesus, even within the Jewish religion. The Pharisees believed in a general resurrection—the righteous to their reward, and the wicked to their punishment. Furthermore, even pagan religions believed in immortality. So in this most common interpretation of the Resurrection, there is nothing uniquely significant about Christ's resurrection. It becomes simply an example of what we already believe, an example of what already awaits all of us.

Another interpretation moves in a somewhat different direction. It sees the Resurrection as an illustration of that life force that moves in all of us, re-creating us, renewing us, sustaining us. The Resurrection becomes a symbol of that flow of life we know in the springtime, which brings dead things back to life. The Resurrection is an example of that which we have felt in our own life when we were down and depressed. Somehow life flows in and picks us up, and we come alive once again.

Claire Randall, General Secretary of the National Council of Churches, speaks of this new life as the power of God's spirit in our lives,

> the power through which we are given the dimension beyond our finite limitations. It is the impetus toward wholeness, and love, and wisdom. I see that spirit and power moving in the new life of individuals and groups that are coming into self-awareness and self-definition, dignity and participation in society. I see it moving to release the new life struggling to be born in a time of transition, as we move from one age to another.[2]

The Resurrection represents, symbolically, the new life bursting forth all around us.

But here, again, Jesus' resurrection is simply an example, one example among any number of other examples that could be chosen. A budding flower in the spring, bursting forth into full bloom, is as good an example of new life as the resurrection of Jesus Christ. In no sense is the resurrection of Christ crucial. In no sense does it speak a unique word that cannot be heard somewhere else.

Probably the most popular interpretation is the one that brings people to church on Easter Sunday as at no other time of the year. Churches are filled to overflowing. Is it because people want to show off their clothes, as some have alleged? Surely, such an allegation is much too superficial. The reason people flock to church on Easter Sunday is because the Resurrection is so often interpreted as part of the American success myth. Nice guys win. Justice triumphs in the end. Goodness comes out on top. Jesus Christ and John Wayne! When we look at the Resurrection in the John Wayne way it sounds like just another success story.

Things were looking pretty grim on Friday. God really had us guessing on Saturday. But Sunday, Easter Sunday, it all turned out just the way we wanted it, so we gather to hear the happy, happy ending. Like Horatio Alger, Jesus Christ triumphed because he stuck to his principles. The hero triumphed, and they all live happily ever after.

Most of us are comforted to know that Christian faith and the American success myth are compatible. We are reassured to know that God is a nice guy who endorses our compulsive need to triumph in whatever we undertake and approves our neurotic need to be successful in everything. But we have added a new twist that even God missed. John Wayne does not have to die to be successful.

There is an infinite number of variations on the American success myth. One was noticed, appropriately, by the *Wall Street Journal*. It featured, as a front page story, a commune which had gathered together under the name MORE. It derived its name from the belief that more could be had by pooling resources.

More teaches that every person is perfect and that, therefore, everything he does is perfect. According to the More philosophy, if a person understands that the only obstacles to his happiness are those he creates himself, the obstacles somehow disappear and he becomes free to seek and get whatever he wants.[3]

We may smile at the naiveté of such a philosophy of life, but, in fact, we are fed and nourished on psychological fads based on this belief. If we can just get in touch with our feelings, we can become beautiful people. If we will just follow Dr. Spock or Dreikurs, we can become better parents. If we will just master a few techniques, we can win friends and influence people. In all these there is the subtle implication that unless we are well-integrated, interesting, creative, successful people who have it all put together, there is something wrong with us. We are not good enough the way we are. We are somehow less than fully human. Something needs to be done to improve on what we are.

The problem with the John Wayne understanding of the Resurrection is that it has nothing to say to the loser. Where is the good word for the person who does not have it all together? What is the gospel for the person who has to die? We stammer in answering. The possibility of losing, much less dying, is simply rank heresy to the American interpretation of the Resurrection. As Vince Lombardi once said, "Winning isn't the main thing, it's the *only* thing." Life is reduced to those times when we win. The times when we lose are to be ignored. Apology and guilt are our reactions to losing. To lose is not really to be alive. Winning is not the main thing; it is the only thing by which life is to be measured.

Who, for example, remembers the runner who came in second in the hundred-yard dash at the last Olympics? He was faster than nearly everyone else in the world. Better than any of us. Yet who was he? No one remembers his name. None cares to remember.

He did not win, so he might as well have come in last for all we care.

The Resurrection, then, is seen as the story of a winner. Jesus may not have gotten his point across during his lifetime, but in the end he was successful. For a while it looked as though the bad guys might win, but now all that can be forgotten. The Cross can be put behind us once and for all because in the closing seconds, Jesus showed everyone who was boss.

Such an interpretation of the Resurrection makes sense within the context of the American success myth. The world is attracted by it. You can sell it in Peoria. Churches are filled by this understanding of the Resurrection.

But Paul contradicts this view directly.

> For the word of the cross is folly to those who are perishing, but to us who are being saved it is the power of God. For it is written, "I will destroy the wisdom of the wise, and the cleverness of the clever I will thwart." Where is the wise man? Where is the scribe? Where is the debater of this age? Has not God made foolish the wisdom of the world?
>
> I Corinthians 1:18

Paul's interpretation of the Resurrection has to do business with the Cross, otherwise it makes no sense at all. The Resurrection is not some statement of general truth. It is not an illustration of eternal life, nor an example of life's automatic buoyancy. It is not an endorsement of success and ambition. The Resurrection, Paul says, makes sense only as we hear it,

*90*

understand it, and wrestle with it in light of the scandalous Cross.

The Resurrection is addressed to those of us who are wrestling with the anguish and awkward embarrassment of the cross. For the followers of Jesus, having their hero die was bad enough, but it was almost unforgiveable to have him die a scandalous death as a common criminal, unacquitted. The significance of the Resurrection can be understood only as we stand, like the followers of Jesus, before the Cross, embarrassed by its foolishness.

The Resurrection, therefore, is God's word about the Cross. The Resurrection is God's word spoken about the Loser! And the Loser is Jesus Christ! The Resurrection is God's word saying, "I approve of the Loser. I like his style." The Resurrection is God's statement about a humanity that is weak and vulnerable and unsuccessful. The Resurrection is not an endorsement of success. It is not an approval of strength. It is an endorsement of the humanity of Jesus Christ, the Crucified One.

Now let us look at him closely—and set aside for a moment our rose-colored glasses. Here is the great faith healer, healing first this one and then that one, only to find that in a matter of months or years all those he helped died anyway.

Here is the great teacher whose words of wisdom are never understood by his disciples. Instead, they constantly ask stupid questions of Jesus until his frustration is too much for them. They cease their questioning only because they are afraid he will snap at them. In the end they desert him because they do not understand the Cross.

Here is the great man of faith, hanging on the Cross, crying out in his doubt, "My God, my God, have You forsaken me?" (paraphrase, Matthew 27:46).

Here is the wonder worker who can turn water into wine or walk on the sea or calm the storm, hanging on the Cross, powerless.

And here is the long-expected king, the one who is going to pull it all together, a failure at the age of thirty-three. All the expectations of his family, his friends, his followers, and the religious experts, were dashed because their hero is a washout.

Across *this* humanity, God writes, "It is good!"

Because the Resurrection is God's word spoken about such humanity, it is God's word spoken about *our* humanity and the ambiguities in which we live out our lives. Weakness is as much a part of life as strength—and it is good! Suffering is as much a part of life as health—and it is good. Failure is as much a part of life as success—and it is good. Doubt is as much a part of life as certainty—and it is good. Fear is as much a part of life as faith—and it has been approved.

In the Resurrection God says, "I give you permission to be human. You do not have to be successful; you do not have to get it all together; you do not have to be the best parent in the world; you do not have to get that promotion. You are accepted. With all your frailty, with all your weakness, with all your vulnerability, I accept you.

God frees us from the bondage of having to be

perfect. He delivers us from the tyranny of our divine ambitions, trying to play god. It is precisely the God who frustrates our compulsive need to be saintly and successful reminding us, time and again, of our vulnerability—in short, God the enemy—who is identified by the Resurrection as the God of grace, the one who gives us permission to live as human beings.

The Cross, so far as the world is concerned, is a symbol of embarrassing failure. But through the spectacles of the Resurrection we see it as God's permission to fail. If the Cross is good enough for God, it is good enough for us. We are freed from the tyranny of having to succeed. We are freed from the neurotic compulsion of having to measure up to somebody else's standards in order to be of worth. To believe in Christ's resurrection is to believe that we have been given permission to be Charlie Browns, and, despite our best intentions, to live with feet of clay. "In the world you will have tribulation," said Jesus. In this world of production standards, social requirements, popular expectations, you will have frustrating reminders of your liabilities and limitations. "But," Jesus continues, "be of good cheer. I have overcome the world" (John 16:33). We are free—free to be human. Free to live with feet of clay, free to fail, and free, ultimately, to die. "To believe in God," says Joseph Pintaure, "is to die and not be embarrassed."

Such an understanding of life fosters good mental health. Over the centuries people have come to realize there is a continual and unavoidable sense of conflict in themselves which cannot be ignored by covering it over with the "beautiful person" label. It is important for us, say psychiatrists, to become aware of these inner conflicts and to recognize them, not as horrible burdens, but rather as opportunities for growth. Sometimes we do grow because of these inner unavoidable conflicts. Sometimes we are defeated by them. But win or lose, we have been approved.

In that magnificent play, *Death of a Salesman,* the wife of Willie Loman talks with her son about the father with whom he has become disenchanted. She tries to explain about the man she loves.

> I don't say he's a great man. Willie Loman never made a lot of money. His name was never in the paper. He's not the finest character that ever lived. But, he's a human being, and a terrible thing is happening to him. So attention must be paid. He's not to be allowed to fall in his grave like an old dog. Attention, attention must finally be paid to such a person.[4]

The Resurrection is God's word that attention has been paid to such a person. God may have other words for other worlds, but his word for this world is "Jesus Christ." Jesus Christ crucified, and Jesus Christ raised from the dead. The two have to go together. The Resurrection is God's commentary on the Crucifixion. The Crucifixion is the symbol of life's vulnerability, its frailties, its weaknesses, its failures. And across it all, God has written his comment, "Approved."

# Recognizing the Devil

Before we explore more fully the meaning of God's permission to live as human beings, we must digress for a bit to look at the reality of the temptor among us.

There has been a good deal of interest recently in the subject of demon-possession and the devil. If box office receipts are any indication, motion pictures such as *The Exorcist* have tapped a growing interest in and a developing concern with the devil's presence. Whatever other liabilities such motion pictures may have, their depiction of the devil obscures his real existence among us. Satan is portrayed as a supernatural power, lurking in Victorian settings, ready to inhabit our bodies and infiltrate our minds. The presence of Satan is betrayed by a peculiar body odor, the smell of brimstone. He causes weird phenomena, such as chairs flying across the room. His presence is something to be feared. Satan lurks in dark corners, ready to overtake us and tempt us. He is obviously evil, and it is clear he should be avoided.

While such a caricature is common and can be traced back to the Middle Ages, it is almost sure to obscure our awareness of the devil's real presence. Just how foreign it is to the biblical understanding of the temptor can be seen in Matthew's story.

> Jesus began to show his disciples that he must go to Jerusalem and suffer many things from the elders and chief priests and scribes, and be killed, and on the third day be raised. And Peter took him and began to rebuke him, saying, "God forbid, Lord! This shall never happen to you." But he turned and said to Peter, "Get behind me, Satan! You are a hindrance to me; for you are not on the side of God, but of men."
>
> (Matthew 16:21-23)

Jesus had just announced to the disciples what he understood to be God's will for his life, namely, suffering and death. Peter—blessed, friendly, comforting Peter—put his arm around Jesus and took him aside to offer assurance, "Jesus, this can never happen to you. You are much too important. You are much too beautiful a person." Peter was trying to comfort Jesus and save him from depression. Nothing supernatural about that. Nothing weird. No obvious evil. We probably would say the same thing. The remarkable and disturbing thing about Matthew's story is that Jesus turned on friendly, comforting, reassuring Peter and said, "Get behind me, Satan!" Jesus recognized the devil right next to him, but not in any way you or I have been led to understand him. Why did Jesus speak of this well-meaning attempt to console him as the voice of Satan?

Consider first that Peter's worthwhile attempt was, nonetheless, tempting Jesus to be disobedient to God's will. The stark fact is that Jesus believed God's will for his life was to die on the Cross. He apparently believed that from the time of his baptism. Certainly, Matthew and the other Gospel writers looking back at the events of Jesus' life thought so. No other understanding of God's will makes sense of their accounts. Neither healing nor performing wonders. Although these activities might have been a reason for living, Jesus, time and again walked away from them and said this was not his major concern. Nor was it teaching. It is remarkable that Jesus never told the disciples to take notes on his teaching. He had no concern to keep a record of what he said, as did the rabbis and prophets before him. Jesus had not the slightest interest in preserving or publishing his material. Nor was Jesus greatly interested in organizing a group that would carry on his work. He spent precious little time developing a hierarchy or assigning roles to his disciples.

No, the Gospels make it clear, Jesus set his face to go to Jerusalem because in Jerusalem he had a date with destiny and death. Jesus lived toward his death. He was not a victim of circumstances, nor was he a tragic hero. He gave up his life. "It is finished," he said. "I have done what it was given me to do. Father, into thy hands I commit my spirit" (paraphrase, John 19:30 and Luke 23:46). Obedience for Jesus was to die offering his life as a sacrifice to God.

Obedience to God is never easy, especially when there are other and more attractive options available. For Jesus the temptations were forceful because they offered more promising alternatives than death. In the Gospel accounts it would be a mistake to picture the devil as some outside force coming to Jesus with a list of temptations. Rather, we need to see Jesus' struggle as an inner one in which he wrestled with other possibilities that made more sense. In the wilderness Jesus could see better options than death. Certainly, it makes more sense to establish a reputation as a wonder worker with a few fast routines, and then lay your message on the folks with a few catchy slogans. The world listens to a Madison Avenue approach. Jesus knew that.

Jesus could see the world's ill and hungry people, for whom he had so much to offer. Feeding the thousands, healing the sick, spending years working at training people to come after him to carry on the work—that makes sense. But not death. Throwing life away is absurd.

Bribery or selling out to effect a worthy end makes more sense. In recent disclosures the respected FBI and CIA, as well as several American business concerns, followed a policy of the end justifies the means; it may not be moral, but it makes sense. But dying? The whole force of Jesus' prayer in Gethsemane and his cry of dereliction on the Cross, "My God, my God, why have you forsaken me?" is that death did not make any sense to him—not as the will of God.

But Jesus worked through his own inner struggle and came to terms with God's mysterious and incomprehensible will. Until good old, well-meaning, thoughtful Peter put his arm around Jesus and said,

"This shall never happen to you." Then the wounds were torn open again. The scabs were ripped away, and Jesus was back in the wilderness, wrestling with those other options. "Get behind me, Satan. I don't want to hear it." The first indication of the devil's presence is that he always comes with a better offer than obedience. He always presents us with an alternative more appealing than what God has in mind. In the garden of Eden story, the temptor comes to Adam and Eve with luscious fruit and the offer, "Eat, it will be good for you. Never mind that God has said it is forbidden."

That brings us to the second sign by which we recognize the devil among us. Temptation is always packaged attractively. Disobedience always appears to be more appealing and sensible than obedience. There is an unforgettable line in Archibald MacLeish's play *J.B.* in which Satan comes to Job sitting amidst the death around him. His family is gone, his goods are gone, his own body wracked by pain and ruined by boils. In the midst of this stench of death comes Satan who whispers to Job:

> J.B.! . . . It's me.
> I'm not the Father.
> I'm the-Friend. . . .
> All I wanted was to
> help. . . ."[1]

The Father God is the one who meets us as the enemy in order that we might know him as the God of grace. He is the one who continually confronts us with our humanity. He is the one who stands behind Job's suffering. But Satan comes to Job with a much more attractive offer—friendship. All he wanted to do was help.

All Satan ever wants to do is help us be something other than human beings who are bounded by time, flawed by weakness, and have the scent of death about us. He nourishes our intoxicating desire to be godlike—rising above our imperfections, transcending any weakness, becoming thereby eternally youthful, forever beautiful, always strong, unquestionably successful, and assuredly in control. We are compulsive writers of fiction and fantasy. But God resists our attempts to write happy endings to life, and thereby appears to be our enemy. The tell-tale evidence by which we recognize the devil is that he comes to us as the friend and never takes death seriously. Satan has a better idea. Peter loved Jesus and said, "Lord, you won't have to die. Surely that isn't what is meant for you. There must be an easier way." Genesis portrays the temptation for Adam and Eve as the offer of life. "You will not die. For God knows that when you eat of it . . . you will be like God" (Genesis 3:4, 5).

There are many words in our world which tell us how beautiful, and strong, and godlike we are and that we need not grow old and die. We hear the words coming at us through television commercials. Grecian Formula, for example, advertises a product that hides the gray hairs—if combed into our scalp it will gradually make us look young again. Beautiful people do not need to look old or be afflicted with the disabilities of age. We hear the words in pulpits, offered in the name of religion. Perhaps one of the best known preachers of our time is Robert Schuller, minister of one of the fastest growing churches in the country—seven thousand members and adding eight hundred new members a year, operating with a budget of four million dollars and with letters of admiration from no less than Doris Day and Hubert Humphrey. *Time Magazine* said,

> Instead of theology, a Schuller sermon is packed with success stories, accented by alliterative slogans and an "I'm okay—you're O.K." philosophy. He calls it "possibility thinking." . . . Good Christians, Schuller intones, are "act-chievers" who "try-umph" over pessimism. "I don't trust skeptics, no matter how brilliant their words," he says. "I trust Jesus. He was the greatest possibility thinker that ever lived."[2]

No wonder his church is growing so rapidly. Who would not want to hear such beautiful and attractive words about our possibilities? But beware the words of the devil, "You shall not die. Put those thoughts far from your mind. I am your friend who brings you a life of victories without defeats. Resurrection without any crosses."

At the end of our possibilities lies an abrupt end. We are limited creatures. We are bounded by birth and by death. We bear the marks of vulnerability from the time we take our first breath. We cannot escape our limitations any more than we can wish them away. We are tempted to get busy with our projects and throw ourselves into our work, tearing down our barns to build bigger ones, so we will not have to think about the limitations life has placed on us. But God says to us, "Fool, this night your soul is required of you" (Luke 12:20). Strong language. But it forces us to recognize what Jonathan Edwards understood so long ago. In the end a person's business is with God. Edwards was no pessimist, but he was a realist. He realized that there is no such thing as cheap grace. There is no escape from life's boundaries, and to live at all is to come to terms with them. To know the God of grace is to have met him as the opponent who says no to our dreams of divinity.

*I Never Promised You a Rose Garden* is the story of a seventeen-year-old mentally ill girl. She is finally taken to a mental hospital where she is confronted with her illness. For the first time a doctor said, "Debbie, you are sick."

"Like the rest of them here?" It was as near as she dared go, already much too near the black places of terror.

"Do you mean to ask me if I think you belong here, if yours is what is called a mental illness? Then the answer is yes. I think you are sick in this way, but with your very hard work here and with a doctor working hard with you, I think you can get better."

As bald as that. Yet, with the terror connected with the hedged-about, circled-around word "crazy," the unspoken word that Deborah was thinking about now, there was a light coming from the doctor's spoken words, a kind of light that shone back on many rooms of the past. The home and the school and all of the doctor's offices ringing with the joyful accusation: There is Nothing the Matter With You. Deborah had known for years and years that there was more than a little the matter—something deeply and gravely the matter. . . . [But] They had always said, "There is nothing the matter with you, if you would only . . ." Here at last was a vindication for all those angers in all those offices.[3]

The good news of our faith is that Jesus takes us seriously in our vulnerability. He takes us seriously as limited people. He takes us seriously as human beings who have the scent of death about us and who carry its marks in our lives. Satan would offer us the consoling word, "There is nothing the matter with you, if only you would . . ." But Christ is the down-to-earth realist who knows that there are no shortcuts to the Resurrection. We go by the way of the Cross, or we do not go at all. Anyone who speaks of grace apart from the Cross is lying. Anyone who speaks of life without taking death seriously is speaking for Satan. And, anyone who talks about wholeness without taking limitations seriously is the voice of the devil. We have the word of Christ on it. He recognized the devil.

# Living with Demons

What does it mean to live as a human being? Answers come from philosophers and poets, motion pictures and Madison Avenue. Everyone, it seems, wants to get into the act. Our image of what being human means is molded for us by the matrix of values and attitudes in which we live. It is shaped by the stories we come to accept as reality.

Some time ago, for example, there was a television commercial advertising a product which, when added to the wash water, was reported to make towels and T-shirts soft and fluffy. One of the advantages of using the product, the commercial implied, was that a teen-ager would run to his mother when he discovered how soft his T-shirts were, and give her a hug saying, "Gee, Mom, I love you." I cannot vouch for the effectiveness of the product in making clothes soft, but I am almost certain that it would have nothing to do with human relations. If the reality is anything like our household, the teen-ager—far from noticing the softness—would complain that he had to go to the dryer to get his T-shirts instead of finding them in his dresser.

The commercial illustrates the difference between myth and reality. What is promised and the fulfillment of the promise are two different things. The Bible reflects this same gap between promise and fulfillment. There, for example, is Joshua, standing on the far side of the Jordan River, ready to lead his people into the Promised Land. He psyches them up with these words: "Hereby you shall know the living God is among you, and that he will without fail drive out from before you the Canaanites, the Hittites, . . . the Perizzites, . . . the Amorites, and the Jebusites" (Joshua 3:10). That was the promise. The reality was something different as the records indicate.

However, they did not drive out the Canaanites that dwelt in Gezer: so the Canaanites have dwelt in the midst of Ephraim to this day but have become slaves to do forced labor. . . .

Manasseh did not drive out the inhabitants of Bethshean and its villages. . . . But the Canaanites persisted in dwelling in that land. When Israel grew strong, they put the Canaanites to forced labor, but did not utterly drive them out.

And Ephraim did not drive out the Canaanites who dwelt in Gezer; but the Canaanites dwelt in Gezer among them.

Zebulon did not drive out the inhabitants of Kitron, or the inhabitants of Nahalol; but the Canaanites dwelt among them, and became subject to forced labor.

Asher did not drive out the inhabitants of Acco, or the inhabitants of Sidon; . . . but the Asherites dwelt among the Canaanites, the inhabitants of the land; for they did not drive them out.

Joshua 16:10; Judges 1:27-32

Several centuries later when Isaiah was looking forward to the coming of the kingdom of God, anticipating the reign of the Messiah, he told the people that the king would heal the diseases of all the people, restoring sight to the blind, enabling the lame to walk, and casting out demons. That was the promise and the expectation.

Reality, however, is painted for us by Mark.

They brought to (Jesus) all who were sick or were possessed with demons. And the whole city was gathered together about the door. And he healed many who were sick with various diseases, and cast out many demons. . . .

And in the morning, a great while before day, [Jesus] rose and went out to a lonely place, and there he prayed. And Simon and those who were with him pursued him, and they found him and said to him, "Every one is searching for you." [But] he said to them, "Let us go on to the next towns, that I may preach there also; for that is why I came."

1:32-38

Jesus apparently had no intention of casting out all the demons: The kingdom of God spoken of by Isaiah turned out, in reality, to be the land where demons not only dwelt, but where the king had no intention of casting them all out.

These stories raise the question, Are we dealing with

a breakdown between the promises of God and their fulfillment? For us the matter has some significance. If that is what the Bible stories indicate, then God is at best a well-intentioned but powerless God who is unable to deliver the goods, or worse, a cruel joker who welches on his word.

What, for example, is the person who believes in faith healing to make of the fact that his prayers for physical recovery go unanswered? Encouraged by Jesus' words and example, he implores heaven for restoration or relief. Yet nothing happens. Too often we have accused the patient for not praying often enough or more fervently. We blame the person's faith rather than admit the possibility that God may be at fault. Richard Rubenstein, author of the disturbing book *After Auschwitz,* argues that it is obscene that a God worthy of human adoration could have inflicted Auschwitz on what was allegedly his people.[1] Certainly the victims raised prayers to God for deliverance. Yet for six million, there was no response. It is inconceivable to Rubenstein that a God who had promised to make of them his people, could have allowed the Canaanites [Nazis] to inhabit the land and to inflict the holocaust upon them. Rubenstein comes to the conclusion, therefore, that God is dead. He chooses to side with Camus, preferring a meaningless universe to a God whose world would have to include the events of the extermination. These stories, plus the others which we could add from our own experience, raise the questions, Is God a cruel tyrant? or perhaps worse, Is he dead?

When we look at Jesus as the embodiment of God's will, however, we can come to quite a different conclusion. We do not see the breakdown between promise and fulfillment, but rather a *miracle,* a miracle of God's grace.

Behold the man! Whatever else we may say about Jesus, he is a man who tells it like it is. Christ says, "In the world you will have tribulation." In the world there are demons. Jesus had no intention of casting them all out because it was an impossibility. Israel discovered the Canaanites were too well entrenched to ever be free of them. At worst, she would have to live with them. At best, they might become her servants. But the miracle of grace is that we can live with the demons and the Canaanites. "In the world you [will] have tribulation, but be of good cheer," Jesus goes on, "I have overcome the world."

The popular myth is that we can begin living only when we have cast out all the demons and gotten rid of the Canaanites. To live as a human being, we are told, means we must be happy and whole. Madison Avenue knows what we need to be human. It offers us the products without which a whole life is inconceivable. Human beings are people with white, sparkling teeth; they smell nice, drive sleek, shiny automobiles on their way to happy homes and prosperous jobs. But what if in reality our jobs are deadly dull or our marriages are on the rocks? Where is wholeness for us if our car is in the garage or the finance company has repossessed it? What if some of our teeth are missing, we sweat a lot, and have bad breath? What does it mean for us to live as human beings?

The reply of Jesus is, "Take up your cross and follow me." He not only assumes that each of us will have a cross, but more remarkably, he assumes *we can bear it*. Rather than have us believe we can get rid of our crosses by earnest prayer or positive thinking, Jesus, who is an expert on crosses, knows that each of us will be assigned one or more. The grace of God is found, not by having them miraculously disappear, but in the discovery that we can, in fact, carry them. The thing that makes Jesus Christ our Savior—the one who frees us to live joyously—is that Jesus learned how to live in the land of the demons. Jesus lived a life under the shadow of the cross, and yet he called life good. He was surrounded by the blundering confusion of his disciples, and yet he was joyous. Jesus was beset by doubts and temptations, yet he was not overcome by them. He constantly wrestled within himself over the meaning of his ministry and life, and yet he never became self-centered. He was betrayed and denied by his closest friends, yet he loved them. When one beholds such a man, one knows, "I am not that man!" One stands in the presence of an impossible humanity that is amazing and awesome. It is a humanity that is only a divine possibility. With the Roman centurion, we look at him and say, "Surely, here is the Son of God" (paraphrase, Matthew 27:54).

To call Jesus Son of God means functionally that what we see in him gives us a clue to what God is like. When we look at him we do not see a cruel joker. When we behold his humanity, we do not see a well-meaning, but inept and powerless God. In him we see the God of grace. The veil of the Enemy is lifted and the God of grace revealed. In Christ we see the amazing ability to live in the land of the Canaanites with the demons and yet be neither defeated nor destroyed by them. In him we see that though we cannot do anything about the arbitrariness of life, we also see that we do not have to. We can accept life as it is and say yes to it because of the one God has made king of his kingdom. The kingdom of God consists in just this: we can live in the same land with the Canaanites and the demons.

Let us look once again at the courage of the seventeen-year-old girl in *I Never Promised You a Rose Garden* who is hospitalized in an institution for the insane. It is sometimes breathtaking as she risks leaving the security of her madness and entering again the world of reality. She recovers sufficiently to leave the hospital, although she will never be as strong as people who have not been mentally ill. Nevertheless, she leaves with a wisdom far exceeding that of those who have never lived in the land of the demons. She learns that mental health is not the absence of depression or problems. It is the ability to cope with them. Mental health is not found by defeating the demons, but in choosing to do battle with them. Again and again the voices within her overpower her, and she is forced to return to the hospital for treatment. But again and again she musters her courage and returns to the world of reality. During one of her stays in the hospital she finds that her fellow inmates resent her presence among them. Indeed, one of them is so angered that she throws a cup at her, hitting her in the head.

> [Debbie] looked again at the faces in the ward. Her presence was making them struggle with Maybes. Suddenly she realized she was . . . a living symbol of hope and failure and the terror they all felt of their own resiliency and hers, reeling punch-drunk from beating after beating, yet, at the secret bell, up again for more. She saw why she could never explain the nature of her failure to these people who so needed to understand it, and why she could never justify scraping together her face and strength to go out again . . . and again.[2]

The miracle of grace is that we go out again and again . . . and yet again to struggle with the demons and fight the Canaanites even though we will *never* defeat them.

Faith in Christ is the conviction that my well-being is not dependent upon winning the battle in which I am engaged. My well-being is not dependent upon driving out the Canaanites whom I come to recognize as a permanent part of the landscape. Rather, faith is the belief that in the battle that I am losing, I do not need to be anxious because I am safe in God's care and keeping. The victory of faith is not in winning the war against the enemy, the Canaanites, but in choosing to do battle with them. In choosing to do battle we deny them their power to define and determine us.

Read again these remarkable words of experience, which the church calls the Word of God and which

*111*

reflect the reality of human life. "Manasseh did not drive out the inhabitants of Bethshean and the villages . . . but the Canaanites persisted in dwelling in that land. When Israel grew strong, they put the Canaanites to forced labor but did not utterly drive them out."

# Tin Cups, Weak Ankles and All That

Now Peter and John were going up to the temple at the hour of prayer, the ninth hour. And a man lame from birth was being carried, whom they laid daily at that gate of the temple which is called Beautiful to ask alms of those people who entered the temple. Seeing Peter and John about to go into the temple, he asked for alms. And Peter directed his gaze at him, with John, and said, "Look at us." And he fixed his attention upon them, expecting to receive something from them. But Peter said, "I have no silver and gold, but I give you what I have; in the name of Jesus Christ of Nazareth, walk." And he took him by the right hand and raised him up; and immediately his feet and ankles were made strong. And leaping up he stood and walked and entered the temple with them, walking and leaping and praising God. And all of the people saw him walking and praising God, and recognized him as the one who sat for alms at the Beautiful Gate of the temple; and they were filled with wonder and amazement at what had happened to him.

Acts 3:1-10

Luke paints a poignant and pathetic picture of a lame man, dependent on others to carry him to the temple

*113*

gate where he has to sit all day in the dust of the street. One day is pretty much as the next. Begging has become a way of life for him. Holding out his tin cup, he depends upon the generosity of those who pass by to throw him a coin. He has long since learned to settle for little and not hope for much. Despair has become a leaden weight that he must endure. The only thing of significance in his life is the sound of coins clinking in his cup.

Into his life one day Peter came. Hardly a memorable beginning for what was to be such an important day. With routine indifference the beggar holds out his cup, gesturing for generosity from the passerby.

How different the ending would have been had Peter given him what he asked for, he would have been happy in his misery. His day would have ended just as it had begun—with the same routine. Nothing would have been changed.

From our perspective, it all seems so obvious. We can see that the beggar was looking for the wrong thing. But if we put ourselves in his place, the farthest thing from our mind would be healing. Of all the things he could have hoped for, being healed was about the last. He had long since come to settle for much less. All he wanted was a few coins from the temple traffic to get him through the day. His only concern with the temple was that it tended to attract generous people. Praising God inside it was not on his agenda.

The Bible is filled with the stories of human desires turned into requests of God, attempts to use him for our own ends. Israel wanted to become a great nation and have her own king. Her ambition was to have all the peoples of the world bow down to her and pay her homage. She wanted her enemies to recognize their foolishness in having opposed her. It was assumed God would approve her plans.

Judas wanted Jesus to be a powerful leader, a man whose greatness would measure up to Judas's specifications and those of the world. He expected Jesus to prove himself and demonstrate his power to the crowd; to throw off the mantle of weakness and humility and flex his messianic muscles.

It is true of us as well. In a thousand ways we hold out our tin cups for God to fill with silver or gold. Our prayers often treat God as a cosmic bellboy to run our errands. We want God to do for us whatever we ask—healing us by faith, helping us get a better job, smoothing out a difficult situation. We demand that our faith be practical.

Out of World War II came the story of General Patton who demanded that his chaplain offer a prayer which would clear away the clouds so that the battle could begin. We are amazed and amused at such a faith. But very often we, too, relate to God in the same way. We want him to approve our agendas. We ask him to remove the threats to our peace of mind. We pray he will heal our diseases. We expect him to answer our questions. If our prayers are not answered, we assume that we have not exercised enough faith or read our Bibles as diligently as we should. Like Linus and Sally, who sit waiting for the Great Pumpkin to appear bringing all kinds of goodies, we look upon God as the Great Benefactor who can be expected to do for us whatever we want. If our requests go unanswered, we assume the fault is in our asking, not in that for which we ask. Surely God will respond to our empty cup, held up in his presence. It never occurs to us to ask for something other than the silver or gold necessary to fill it. After all, who should know better than we what is needed to live?

Into such a situation Luke thrusts the Word of God, "Silver and gold have I none." We, like the beggar, are asking for the wrong thing. We want life on our terms, but we encounter the Enemy who has a different agenda than ours. The Word addresses us by saying no! The name of the game is not silver and gold; the name of the game is not peace of mind; nor happiness; nor success.

The Cross is God's response to our petitions. The New Testament does not picture the Crucifixion's overtaking Jesus as a hapless victim. Rather, it portrays Jesus as one who "set his face" toward Jerusalem to stand trial willingly. The New Testament boldly presents the Crucifixion as God's will for Christ and, therefore, for us as well. "If any man would come after me," says Jesus, "let him deny himself and take up his cross and follow me" (Matthew 16:24). The Cross stands as the Enemy's *no* written across all our desires to be successful; to live long, happy, peaceful lives. It puts an end to our attempts to beg a living on our own terms.

This is not to suggest that the Cross is some evil

thing, nor is it to suggest that God is some kind of monster who gets sadistic pleasure from denying our desires. The Cross is simply reality. It is the truth about us. It is God's commentary on our humanity. We are finite creatures. Our joys fade. Our health fails. Our days come to an end. Whatever else can be said of biblical faith, it is realistic. It takes us seriously as vulnerable people who bear the marks of weaknesses and the scent of death. It takes us seriously in our inadequacies, even as it took this beggar seriously as a cripple. The Word came to him as it comes to us in our situation and addresses us as we are. "I have no silver and gold coins, but I give you what I have. Cripple, in the name of Jesus Christ, get up and walk."

This story is remarkable because it is not a healing miracle of Jesus. The healing is accomplished by Peter. Peter is the one who speaks the words. It could have been Matthew or Luke or you or me. The *power*, however, is in the name of Jesus Christ.

This is important to remember since none of us has ever seen Jesus in the flesh. None of us has ever heard him speak. We have all received our faith by hearing of him in name only. The change we have experienced in our life because of that faith has been brought about by the power of his story as it has been told to us. That is the power that Luke is speaking of, the power that changed the life of that lame beggar, and the power that can change lives today.

I have seen people pick up the broken pieces of their lives with a radiancy and a sense of buoyancy nothing less than miraculous. Returning to a situation that

*117*

would normally be thought of as overwhelming and desperate, they are able to go on as victors rather than victims. With the power of Jesus' name I have seen people face crisis after crisis and face each with a sense of confidence. "I can do all things through him who strengthens me," said Paul (paraphrase Philippians 4:13).

We may wonder what is the power in His name? It is the power of His story. Jesus was more than simply a good teacher or a great person. His significance is not merely as a wonder worker. Jesus Christ was the one whom God raised from the dead! The power in the name of Christ is the power of the resurrection story. The claim that we are invited to entertain is that Christ has overcome death and, therefore, Christ has overcome all limitations to human life.

The claim gives us divine permission to accept our lives as they are. The power of the resurrection story is that it calls us to face our inadequacies and our limitations and take them seriously without being defined and determined by them. We are cripples, yes. We are limited people, yes. We are weak people, yes. We are disposed to illness, yes. We are doomed to die, yes. And these limitations define us, no! To live by the power of Jesus' name is to live by the power of God who refuses to allow limitations, weaknesses, and death to define us. To live by the power of Jesus' name is to live by the belief that if the God of grace is for us, no limitation can be against us. We may be crushed, but we are not destroyed. We may be discouraged, but we are not left hopeless. We may be bereaved, but we are not reduced to despair.

I may be neurotic, but my neurosis does not need to make me feel guilty. I may be ill, but my illness does not have the power to define me. I may not be able to speak or love with the ability of angels, but that disability does not deter me from speaking or loving as best I can.

In a situation similar to the one in which Peter found himself, Jesus said to a lame beggar, "Rise, take up your pallet, and walk" (John 5:8). We might amplify his words, "Stop waiting around for your ship to come in. Stop wasting your time hoping for illusions. Take up your infirmity and start living. You have been here all your life, and all you know are these surroundings and the people who come here with crumbs for you. There is a whole world in which to live and a whole life to be experienced. You do not need to be healed to start living. Take up your pallet and walk. Bring it with you, but get moving!" The remarkable words of Isaiah come to mind, "In the wilderness there shall be springs of water. In the desert there shall be streams" (paraphrase, Isaiah 35:6). To one man Jesus said, "Take up your pallet and walk," but to all of us he says, "Take up your crosses and come follow me into the great adventure of living."

But the power of the Resurrection claim goes farther. It is not just that we have been given permission to live our lives with all their limitations and weaknesses. This, too, the Stoic and Cynic can do. It is rather that the resurrection story gives us permission to rename our experiences. We are not locked into the names that have been attached to us. The labels that have been pasted across our lives are not fixed. The Enemy who confronts us with crosses is seen as the God of grace when he places the spectacles of the resurrection story on our eyes. Grace is God's permission to rename our lives. The world, for example, looks at the Cross and labels it: Failure—Scandal—Embarrassment—Dead End—Tragedy—Death. the resurrection of Jesus is God's invitation to rename it. God is saying, "You don't have to live with those categories." The Resurrection gives us permission to name the Cross as a symbol of life, not death. It gives us permission to call the Cross a symbol of glory, not scandal. A symbol of atonement, not dead end. New beginnings, not failure. The Cross is not eradicated but, when we rename it, everything in life is seen differently. Christian hope is not something we derive from the evidence. Christian hope is something we claim contrary to the evidence and only because God gives us permission to draw contrary conclusions —to rename the data.

Jesus' whole style of relating to life was based on this kind of inversion. He came into a world where the categories had all been predetermined. The rich were to be noticed. The powerful were in control. The religious were going to be rewarded, and the sinners were out of luck. Into that kind of set, closed world, Jesus came and said that the poor are blessed for they shall inherit the earth—not the rich. The sinner will enter the kingdom of God ahead of the religious folk.

To those who had life all figured out, he said, losing your life is the way to find it. And if you try to save it, you will lose it!

One of the clichés of our culture is Love is blind, but marriage is an eye-opener. Not so! Love sees with amazing clarity. Just as love sees the person that can be, so Christ looks at us with amazing clarity, and sees the person that can be. He looked at reckless Peter and saw boldness, so he named him Rock and said, "On this rock I will build a church." Christ does not change us, he renames us. That is a crucial distinction. He does not do away with our neuroses. He simply renames them and calls them gifts, our contribution to life. He does not remove our failures, he calls them new beginnings to life. He does not wipe away our mistakes, he says that is how wisdom is fashioned from life. He does not deliver us from our handicaps, he calls them assets for living. And, most assuredly, he does not deliver us from our weaknesses, but rather calls them strengths to be shared as a part of life.

Perhaps the most important function of faith is not to save souls and get us through the pearly gates—though it may do that—or to impart some divine knowledge that is unavailable elsewhere—though it may do that too. The most significant thing our faith does is give us permission to rename our lives. And, in so doing, be created anew. John Gardner sees the inversion of grace as a series of great opportunities—cleverly disguised as insoluable problems.

Life does not promise us a bed of roses. It does not even promise us justice or fairness. Life does not promise us healing, and it does not promise us deliverance from our burdens. The one thing it promises it does deliver. A variety of experiences. It is the Jesus story that promises us growth: the ability, not only to cope with those experiences life delivers, but permission to rename those experiences as grace-full. The power of Jesus' name does not turn the clock backward, or rerun the film of life to a point where we can pick it up as it once was. The power in his name is the power of God's grace, which confronts us with the possibilities of life, lived with whatever the circumstances may be, and enables us to see them as miraculous opportunities. Life promises only struggle, but the God of grace promises help in that struggle to live and grow and to be amazed.

We, like the beggar, may have an unsolvable problem. But our real problem is that we have such a pitifully meager expectation of life. We sit outside the courts of God's presence willing to settle for a few coins, begging him to fit into our expectations. We sit on our weak ankles and hold out our cup, but God addresses us by saying, "No, silver and gold I do not have. But that which I have I give to you. In the name of Jesus Christ, Cripple, get up and walk. Come inside and celebrate."

"You with the temper, get up and walk. You with your neurosis, get up and run. You with all of your inadequacies, get up and start living. You with the excuses, stop sitting by the side of the road, watching life go by. You who will one day die, exercise your being today. Get up and dance in the name of Christ. Temples are for praising and raging, not begging."

God does not give us silver and gold coins. He gives us something far more important—he gives us, through Jesus Christ, the power to live the life that has been given to us. He gives us power to walk and to dance in spite of our weakness. He gives us power to love and share in spite of our selfishness. He gives us power to celebrate and live in spite of our dying.

# Twenty Thousand Days, More or Less

Lord, thou hast been our dwelling place
  in all generations.
Before the mountains were brought forth,
  or ever thou hadst formed the earth and the world,
  from everlasting to everlasting thou art God.

Thou turnest man back to the dust,
  and sayest, "Turn back, O children of men!"
For a thousand years in thy sight
  are but as yesterday when it is past,
  or as a watch in the night.

Thou dost sweep men away; they are like a dream,
  like grass which is renewed in the morning:
in the morning it flourishes and is renewed;
  in the evening it fades and withers.

For we are consumed by thy anger;
  by thy wrath we are overwhelmed.
Thou has set our iniquities before thee,
  our secret sins in the light of thy countenance.

For all our days pass away under thy wrath,
  our years come to an end like a sigh.

The years of our life are threescore and ten,
  or even by reason of strength fourscore;
yet their span is but toil and trouble;
  they are soon gone, and we fly away.

Who considers the power of thy anger,
  and thy wrath according to the fear of thee?
So teach us to number our days
  that we may get a heart of wisdom.
                              Psalm 90:1-12

This psalm is interesting because although the author knows who his opponent is—that is, the one who has sentenced him to death—he no longer regards him as the Enemy. It is not that the psalmist has become resigned to his fate, but rather that he realized the necessity of working with God to get the most out of his brief lifetime. He has learned how to live with God and to dance with him as partner.

One day, before long, the Enemy will have his way in our lives. You and I will die. What more is there to say?

Probably very little. Until recently, death was a subject about which we did not talk. It was as if it were taboo. Death was surrounded by a conspiracy of silence. Even yet the funeral industry does its best to convince us that death is an illusion. As we have seen, interpreters of the Christian faith sometimes make light of death by insisting that it is not real. The Resurrection is proof of life after death. The Resurrection, therefore, negates death in such a way that we do not have to take death seriously. As a result, we are left to our own resources to make of this inevitable fact of human existence whatever we can.

Sometime ago I was talking with a patient in the hospital who said, "I am dying, and I don't know how to act." Just as we often do not know what to do with our feelings of rage against God because the church has not given us permission to feel them, so we do not know how to act in the face of death because of the conspiracy of silence about it. Because we do not know what to say about it, we usually remain silent. Sometimes we pretend.

Not surprisingly, therefore, we have come to some unfortunate conclusions with regard to death and dying. For one thing, most of us regard death as a terrible thing, something to be avoided at all costs. Thus, when a Martin Luther King, Jr., is assassinated, we say, "Isn't that awful. What a terrible loss."

Others of us are fascinated by death. Sigmund Freud called this fascination the death wish. But we do not have to become psychoanalytical to see evidence of this fascination all around us. The box office proceeds of movies which deal with death and violence are ample proof.

Still others have romanticized death and have portrayed it as the great friend of life. For example, Kahlil Gibran, in his collection of poems *The Prophet* portrays death as a boat that slips silently into harbor and bears us gently out to sea when life is over.

But across this beautiful romanticizing about death, across this morbid fascination with death, across our fear of dying is scratched the inevitable reality of your death and mine. What more is there to say? The Bible has a good deal more to say. Let us stand on this side of the Resurrection and look at death.

The first thing the Bible says is that death is a fact of human existence and, therefore, has to be taken seriously. Too often Christians have not taken death seriously. We have looked at death from the viewpoint of the Resurrection and have drawn the conclusion that death has been negated. In the Resurrection death is destroyed and becomes nothing more than an inconvenient interruption in an otherwise eternal life. The Resurrection is the proof of life after death. We consider ourselves immortal, which is another way of saying invincible. The end result of such thinking is that we never really have to take ourselves seriously as vulnerable creatures. The boundary of death is rarely considered because it is made inconsequential by virtue of the Resurrection.

By contrast the Bible presents the Resurrection as the event that helps us understand the meaning and significance of death. This event invites us to take death seriously. It reminds us that it was Christ who died. The Resurrection emphasizes that death was a reality for Jesus Christ.

Jesus' death would scarcely have received a second glance, and certainly would not have been remembered by the church, had it not been for the Resurrection. It would have been tragic but not unusual. The Resurrection underscores the significance of Jesus' death, underlines the truth that if Jesus, as the Son of God, could not escape death, then neither can we. If he had to take death seriously, so must we. If death was God's will for Christ, so is it his will for us. After the faith healings, after the reprieves from death developed by medical technology, comes the final will of God for all of us, death. In the end we must all reckon with our Enemy who opposes our desire to be invincible.

If we are to live, therefore, we must learn to understand ourselves as limited and finite creatures. Death is not merely a phenomenon marking the end of earthly existence. It is the event which forces us to confront the meaning of our existence prior to death. Thus the psalmist says, "Teach us to number our days that we may apply our hearts unto wisdom." Because we have twenty thousand days, more or less, we must seriously consider what to do with them.

A second thing the Bible assumes about death when viewed from this side of the Resurrection is that there is grace-full wisdom in death.

Death may come by chance, but its reality is not coincidence. Death is God's idea. Its reality is by design. Death is the will of God for us all as human beings. It is our defining characteristic; thus death must have meaning for us as human beings.

We can speak of the wisdom, or meaning of death by drawing an analogy from the arts. A painting by Picasso, for example, has influence only when it is given concreteness by the artist. As long as the painting exists only in his mind as an idea, it can never be enjoyed by the world. As long as it is a painting in the process of being painted, it can never influence humanity. But once it is finished and the idea has been made definite, once the idea has beginning and ending on a canvas, then, and only then, can it have significance.

The same can be said of a symphony or a motion picture. As long as we are listening to a symphony or viewing a film, we do not talk about it. Only when the symphony has been completed by the orchestra and the movie ended, do we discuss its meaning or merits. Only when an art form has made its statement, can we respond.

Like a work of art or a piece of music, a human life must be definitive before it can become truly influential. Death gives human life such definiteness. Human life has beginning and ending, and that enables us to establish ourselves as a definite identity and thus to have influence in time and history on others.

James Meredith spoke of black leadership in the fifties and sixties as understanding this wisdom in death.

To understand the tenor of the '50s and the '60s, you have to understand the great importance of death. Death, and the threat of death, shadowed the life of every leader, North or South. It was a reality. In a sense, it was even a tactic—often a goal.

Martin Luther King and Malcolm X, for example, wanted to die. For each of these men, violent death was the only sure way to preserve their legacy. Each of these men was a moral leader, and such leaders must realize early in their lives, as did Christ, that the best way to accomplish a moral objective is to die right.[1]

Death is what gives meaning to life. Death gives a specific meaning to a particular life. Only after his death, could the life of Martin Luther King, Jr., be assessed and become truly influential. Only after his assassination, could the meaning of his life be wrestled with by the human race. Only as his life became memorable, did it become a legacy that could be launched into history.

There is, then, a wisdom in death. It gives our life definiteness and therefore launches its significance into memory where it can influence others.

To understand death in this manner is to see there is an ethical imperative implied. Because death makes a life memorable, life is to be lived for a purpose. Our lives are to be lived so as to create a worthwhile memory. The cross of Christ calls us to ask the question, "If I am to die eventually, for what might I be remembered? If I must someday cease to exist, how might my days be invested?"

One of the reasons that the fifties and the sixties were so significant for black liberation was that black leadership had a purpose for living. James Meredith was the first black student to attend the University of Mississippi. His enrollment was both risky and epic-making.

During my duty in Japan, . . . my wife and I made the decision of our lives: to return to Mississippi and try and straighten things out. My best contribution, as a person, I felt, would be to enroll as a student at the University of Mississippi.

People still think I was crazy to have done that. "Man, I

never could have done what you did," they'll come up and say. "I would never have had the nerve." I won't deny that there were times, many times, when I did know fear. But I also had a mission to accomplish, so my biggest fear was not the fear of dying but of failure to accomplish the mission I had set for myself.[2]

Death reminds us that we each have a mission. Life is to be lived for a reason. Death calls to our attention that we do not have all the time in the world to invest our years for some purpose. Death, therefore, is not to be seen as a contradiction of such obvious tokens of God's love and goodness as family and friends and good health. Rather, suffering and death are to be understood as essential symbols of life's meaning. They remind us of our finitude and the boundaries of beginning and ending in which we are to establish our identity. They remind us that our life will be definite and, therefore, can be lived for a purpose.

To be interrupted in our daydreams of being superman by the enemy God is to be brought to our senses so that we can see God as grace-full and, therefore, as partner for living the miracle of our lives.

Thus the psalmist asks God to establish the work of his hands. That is, he wants his life to count for something significant, something worth remembering. The earnest thought of death, Soren Kierkegaard reminds us, is life's greatest ally. To see death as real is to see life as an opportunity for creating a significant memory.

The words of a man, sent to Mayo Clinic in Rochester with what was believed to be an incurable disease, were reported in *The Christian Century*. The examination at Mayo's indicated that his illness was not immediately terminal. Thus he said:

> The doctors have given me a comparatively clean bill of health. There is still a future before me . . . the future is yet to be carved out. And I am one of the carvers, however small my part in the great design.
>
> Yes, now that I am reprieved for a time, I am ready to commit myself anew to the kingdom of God . . . For now, more than ever before, I feel a Power and Presence which enable me to live with the inevitable and dare the worthwhile. I'll risk being wrong. And if I am right in trusting, Olé, Jesus![3]

The Resurrection reminds us not only that there is a life to be lived in heaven, but also—and more important for now—there is a life to be lived here. Looking at death and dying from this perspective enables us to dare the worthwhile, and succeeding or failing, it enables us to shout, "Olé, Jesus!"

# God Remembers

O Lord, my God, I call for help by day;
I cry out in the night before thee.
Let my prayer come before thee,
    incline thy ear to my cry!

For my soul is full of troubles,
    and my life draws near to Sheol.
I am reckoned among those who go down to the Pit;
    I am a man who has no strength,
like one forsaken among the dead,
    like the slain that lie in the grave,
like those whom thou dost remember no more,
    for they are cut off from thy hand.

    Remember not the sins of my youth, or my
        transgressions;
    according to thy steadfast love remember me,
    for thy goodness sake, O Lord!

                                    Psalm 88:1-5, 25:7

In the last chapter we talked about the memory that
our life creates. Now we want to explore what happens
when our partner for living, God, remembers it.

    It is important that we enter into the experience of

the psalmist for unless we do, we shall have difficulty hearing the good news. The psalmist knows the seriousness of the situation. He is drawing near to death. He is on the threshold of *extinction*.

Unfortunately, that fact is difficult for us to grasp. When Elizabeth Kübler-Ross first initiated her seminar on death and dying at Chicago Theological Seminary, one of the student-participants reported:

> The idea of meeting someone who is going to die, who knew, and who was waiting for *it* to happen—that terrified me. It is almost as if those people were of a different species than I. Sentence has been passed on them, they knew something that I did not, they were living in a world of expectations different from my own.[1]

It is difficult, therefore, to appreciate the psalmist's situation.

Tolstoy, in speaking of the death of Ivan Illych, gives us some understanding of what it may be like.

> Iván Illých saw that he was dying, and he was in continual despair.
>
> In the depth of his heart he knew he was dying, but not only was he not accustomed to the thought, he simply did not and could not grasp it.
>
> The syllogism he had learned from Kiezewetter's Logic: "Caius is a man, men are mortal, therefore, Caius is mortal," had always seemed to him correct as applied to Caius, but certainly not as applied to himself. That Caius—man in the abstract—was mortal, was perfectly correct, but he was not Caius, not an abstract man, but a creature quite, quite separate from all others. He had

been little Ványa, with a mamma and a papa, with Mitya and Volódya, with the toys, a coachman and a nurse . . . What did Caius know of the smell of that striped leather ball Ványa had been so fond of? Had Caius kissed his mother's hand like that, and did the silk of her dress rustle so for Caius? . . . "Caius really was mortal and it was right for him to die; but for me, little Ványa, Iván Illych, with all my thought and emotions, it's altogether a different matter. It cannot be that I ought to die. That would be too terrible."[2]

Too terrible? Yes! The psalmist contemplates his death as a terrible thing.

But why should we recoil from the contemplation of our death? This feeling of revulsion is by no means universal. Those people who live close to nature are able to accept death as a matter of fact. They are able to accept it as a natural part of human existence. Indeed, as we have said, poets like Kahlil Gibran portray death as a ship that slips silently into harbor, picks up its passenger, and then calmly and beautifully moves out to sea in the cool of evening.

The psalmist lived close to nature. He was also a poet. Yet his feelings are quite different. He faces death and sees it as a terrible thing. Not a natural part of life at all. The reason for his distress is that his understanding of death is connected with sin. In the Bible, from Genesis to Revelation, sin and death go together. Sin, like death, means separation from God. Death, like sin, alienates the psalmist from the goodness of life. He knows that both are destructive to his humanity. Both are a threat to the enjoyment of life, but in death the destruction to life's goodness is irreparable. Death erases his identity.

For this poet there was something sacred about personal identity. This belief in the sacredness of human personality came from the Hebrew belief that God himself was personal. Unlike the Greeks who saw God in abstract, conceptual terms such as "love" and "truth," "wisdom," and "justice," and unlike the Egyptians and Babylonians who portrayed their gods with naturalistic symbols, the Hebrews spoke of God in personal categories. Indeed, he had a proper name, Yahweh. He was a God capable of entering into a personal relationship with his people, a covenant relationship. It was in the give-and-take of this relationship, with its dancing and wrestling, its praising and raging, that the people of the Bible came to understand that God and human kind are more alike than different. The most amazing assertion about this similarity and, therefore, the sacredness of human personality is found in the Genesis story of creation where the writer declares that human beings, and human beings alone, are created in the image of God. Throughout the Bible, from first page to last, the assertion is made: there is something very special about the integrity of human personality, something uniquely godlike about it.

In one way or another most of us have discovered this truth for ourselves. People are important in an ultimate way. There are few *things* in life that really matter. Most of the things we have we could do without. We must have certain commodities to exist, and we value them greatly when they are in short supply. But people matter most. We know that we need food and water to live, but when a loved one dies, we are made acutely aware that people make life *worth* living. Something very important has been taken from us, a relationship which mattered. Our life and humanity are diminished by the loss. In the final analysis, what matters in life is human relationships— People who need people. It is a gift of grace to be a person who needs people. More than merely existing, we are alive when we love and are loved.

Thus we meet our death not so much with a sense of fear as with a kind of nostalgic regret. Like the psalmist, we realize something terrible is happening. In death I am being deprived of the miracle of my existence. I am to be extinct. No one will weep over my death as I will. No one can appreciate the loss as much as I.

I recall years ago when I thought I was having a heart attack. Lying by the side of the road in the lake country of England, near Keswick, I looked up at the mountains that had been there for eons of time and had witnessed the coming and going of countless generations. Now I thought they were witnessing my passing. I remember very vividly looking into the face of death and seeing, not a horrible mask, but a face of total indifference. All my reasons for living were ignored. That my daughter Christie had just been born and that I wanted to enjoy her made no difference to death. That I had just been appointed to the faculty of Illinois College and was looking forward to teaching was of no consequence to death. That I had just been accepted into the doctoral program at San Francisco Seminary and was excited to begin my work was of no concern to death. I wanted these things so much to be a part of my life. But death yawned and was bored. Death was uninterested in my reasons for living.

The psalmist views death as an alien, an unwanted guest invited only by the Enemy, as an unnatural intruder, rather than a friend to be welcomed. Jesus shares the psalmist's view. In Gethsemane he cries out, "Lord, I don't want to die. If there be some other way out of this, any other way, let this cup pass from me" (paraphrase, Mark 14:36). As one who has come to know the awesome miracle of human existence, as one who has come to understand the integrity of each individual personality, especially his own, the psalmist cries out in the face of his extinction, "O God, *remember* me." The poet has worked through his rage at the finality of death and moved beyond mere acquiescence to its inevitability. He has come to know the God of grace who stands behind the miracle of his life and, therefore, with neither desperation nor with any sense of claim upon God, he calls out from need to grace, "O God, remember me."

His plea leads us to wonder, "Is there any reason to hope that such a prayer will be heard? What would it mean for God to remember us?" I want to suggest that the Bible answers in the affirmative and presents the resurrection of Christ as God's remembering.

After the death of Jesus, which was the extinction of the miracle of his life, God remembered and in the remembering, re-created him. That *thought* of God, expressed in the creative Word, which brought all life into being—and God said . . . and it was so—now brought that specific person into being again by remembering him. Re-creation is God's creative thought remembered. God remembers and it is so. When God remembers us we are re-created. It is resurrection. Jesus' resurrection is the guarantee, but resurrection itself is an inevitable consequence of the biblical view of the sacredness of human individuality.

As noted earlier, it is unfortunate, but true, that whenever the Resurrection is discussed, it is usually talked about in terms of resuscitation, a dead body coming back to life. Because we live in a scientific age when such things are "impossible," we tend to dismiss the accounts of it from serious consideration. Decay and decomposition are the facts of life and death. We already know what happens to the brain cells if they are deprived of oxygen too long. There is no possibility of a dead body's being gathered together again in its molecular structure and being able to breathe and function again.

Some theologians even argue against a life after death because our knowledge of biology makes belief in such an existence impossible. Rudolf Bultmann, for one, contends that the Resurrection is really a mythical way of sharing the disciple's awareness that Jesus' complete trust in God, including his willingness to die, is really what living is all about. Resurrection, he contends, refers, not to the resuscitation of a dead corpse, but to the meaning of life as trust and obedience.[3] Since resuscitation is not seen as a viable understanding of the Resurrection, many Christians have dismissed a belief in life after death as foolish or meaningless.

I remember discussing life after death with a friend who contended that it was biologically impossible. It was obvious that neither of us was convincing the other. Finally my friend said, "Well, McClelland, when we die, one of us will be massively surprised."

But why surprised? Is there something incongruous about belief in life after death and biblical faith? I think not. I have already suggested that the Resurrection is an inevitable consequence of biblical concept of individual personality. How are we to make sense, for example, of that thief's words to Jesus on the cross, "Lord, remember me when you come into your kingdom." And Jesus' reply, "Today you will be with me in Paradise" (paraphrase, Luke 23:42, 43)? What does the "you" and "me" mean? Somehow there has to be an integrity about the you-ness and the me-ness that carries over beyond death.

So the question becomes, "Is there some way of conceptualizing the Resurrection other than resuscitation?" Our psalm suggests one—remembering.

We do not have many examples of resuscitation, which makes it difficult to conceive of the Resurrection in those terms. But we do have experiences of remembering. Remembering is an exceedingly powerful dynamic in human life. Anyone who has ever been under hypnosis or who has, with the aid of a therapist, recalled some long-forgotten event, knows the freeing power of remembering the past. Anyone who has ever remembered a friend or a long-dead loved one knows the comfort and power that remembering brings for meeting a troubled situation or facing a new day. Remembering re-creates a past event or a person's presence. Remembering brings the past actively and influentially into the present. Paul calls his friend Timothy to "remember Jesus Christ, risen from the dead" (II Timothy 2:8); Paul believes that in remembering Jesus there is power for living now in the present moment.

More importantly, the Bible speaks of God as remembering. When God remembers, saving events occur! "God remembered Noah in his distress" (paraphrase, Genesis 8:1), and things began to happen. The flood subsided, livable land reappeared, and Noah was saved from his entombment in the ark. In Exodus 2:23-24 the author speaks of God seeing his people in bondage in Egypt and remembering his covenant with them. He called forth Moses, championed the Hebrew's cause, and freed them from their captivity. "Our hope is that God remembers us in our low estate" (paraphrase, Psalm 136:23). Thus the psalmist, as he faces his extinction—the desecration of his being—and the profaning of the miracle of his individuality, cries out to the Savior God—the God of grace—"Lord, remember me!"

Paul, who stands on this side of the Resurrection, affirms the psalmist's faith, "I am sure that neither death nor life, nor angels, nor principalities, nor things present, nor things to come, nor powers, nor height;

nor depth, nor anything else in all creation, will be able to separate us from the love of God in Christ Jesus our Lord" (Romans 8:38-39). Paul is not dealing in rhetoric. He is speaking, rather, as one who knows the sacredness of human personality in its individuality and who, in his encounter with the risen Christ, has seen that sacredness honored and upheld. It is not superstition, nor is it wishful thinking that leads Paul to exclaim: "Death is swallowed up in victory. O death, where is thy victory? O death, where is thy sting? . . . Thanks be to God who gives us the victory through our Lord, Jesus Christ" (I Corinthians 15:54-55, 57). It is because Paul, a more astute theologian than many of us, believes that the Resurrection is the inevitable consequence of a grace-full God who remembers the sacredness of personality and who will, therefore, remember the miracle of our life.

An understanding of the Resurrection as re-creation through God's act of remembering may not solve all the theological questions that arise from our searching minds. But it certainly avoids the biological problem of resuscitation. More importantly, it is confirmed by our experience. The concept of resurrection becomes believeable for us because we have at times known firsthand the creative power of remembering. More-over, we have experienced in our own lives, grace-full moments and events that affirm the miraculous and sacred character of our being. Our experience with life becomes a peg on which to hang the hat of our faith in God. Ours is a God who remembers us. He appreciates and values the miracle of our lives even more than we do. There is one who will weep at our passing more than we; it is God. And that is why he remembers us. And that is why Paul says, "If we live, we live to the Lord, and if we die, we die to the Lord; so then, whether we live or whether we die, we are the Lord's" (Romans 14:8). God calls us into life and sets before us death. He meets us as the Enemy so that we may learn to dance with him as the God of grace through the night and into the dawn of a new day.

# He Calls Us by Name

Hear, you deaf;
   and look, you blind, that you may see! . . .
This is a people robbed and plundered,
   they are all of them trapped in holes
   and hidden in prisons;
they have become a prey with none to rescue,
   a spoil with none to say, "Restore!" . . .
Who gave up Jacob to the spoiler,
   and Israel to the robbers?
Was it not the Lord, against whom we have sinned,
   in whose ways they would not walk,
   and whose law they would not obey?
But now thus says the Lord,
   he who created you, O Jacob,
   he who formed you, O Israel:
"Fear not, for I have redeemed you;
   I have called you by name, you are mine.
When you pass through the waters I will be with you;
   and through the rivers, they shall not overwhelm you;
when you walk through fire you shall not be burned,
   and the flame shall not consume you.
For I am the Lord your God,
   the Holy One of Israel, your Savior."

Isaiah 42:18, 22, 24; 43:1-3

Kurt Vonnegut has written some marvelous lines in *Cat's Cradle:*

> God made mud . . .
> God got lonesome . . .
> So God said to some mud, "Sit up!" . . .
> "See all I've made," said God, "the hills,
> the sea, the sky, the stars." . . .
> And I was some of the mud that got to sit up
> and look around . . .
>
> "Lucky me, lucky mud."[1]

Being grateful to be alive is a good place to conclude our discussion of God who meets us as the enemy in order to be seen as our creator and savior. It is God who calls us into being. It is God who calls us by name and thereby gives designation to our being.

To the Hebrew, a name was the sound of a person's being. It indicated the character of the bearer. We, for example, give the nickname "Slim" to someone with a very slender build or "Red" to a person with matching hair. To the Hebrew the name "Jacob" meant a person who overstepped his limits, a kind of con artist. "Israel" meant one who wrestled with God.

Significantly, the Hebrews also believed that God had a name, "Yahweh." It comes from an obscure Hebrew verb form which seems to mean, "I will cause to be whatever I cause to be." But the name gives us a clue to the nature of God. It seems to suggest that whatever is caused to be is of God. Everything that happens in life is of God. Life is the glove of God's hand.

In good times, that is easy to believe. When things are going well, business is great, and the children are healthy, singing praises to the Great Benefactor from whom all blessings flow comes naturally. But when the times are not so benevolent and circumstances go against us, dare we say that this, too, is of God?

This was exactly the question that faced Isaiah. Israel had been sold into slavery. She was an exiled people. Life had been reduced to drab despair. One day was pretty much as the next, a meaningless and absurd thing. Life had become a painful reminder day after day that she was a failure. She had not been able to deliver the goods as God had required of her. She was a poor excuse for an elect people. She was not good enough. Doubts were raised from within and recriminations from without. She felt as if she were utterly worthless.

Into that situation Isaiah sounded the astounding assertion that God was in the midst of her pain. Yahweh had brought on her trouble. The Great Adversary was the author of her despair. "Who gave up Jacob to the spoiler, and Israel to the robbers? Was it not the Lord, against whom we have sinned, in whose ways they would not walk, and whose laws they would not obey?" Isaiah was saying that God was using these hard times to discipline his people.

Now, to conclude that God is vengeful and vindictive, and that, like a stern father, he had turned Israel over his knee to spank her, is to miss Isaiah's point. Indeed, such a conclusion is rejected by the Book of Job. Whatever else Job may have to say about his encounter with God the enemy, punishment as an explanation for trouble is dismissed. There is, in fact, a difference between punishment and discipline. The former has to do with venting vengeance. Its focus is on the one punishing, while discipline has to do with learning and focuses on the one being guided. Pain and trouble may come for reasons that we cannot understand but the point in Job is the same as in Isaiah. God, for whatever reason, is in the midst of our suffering. God is in the midst of our pain. God is in life, both its joy and sorrow, its sickness and health, its plenty and its want. Only when we understand Isaiah's assertion that God is in life as a hand is in a glove, can we hear the good news he proclaims for God. "Fear not, therefore, I who am life itself, I who give you your life, both its joy and pain, I who call you into being will, therefore, sustain you. I say to you, do not fear life."

Many of us spend a good deal of time doing just that, fearing life. By fear I do not mean the kind that causes us to lock doors or look under the bed. I am referring to the kind of fear that causes us, as a people, to consume tons of tranquilizers, to suffer from ulcers, and to die of heart attacks. I am talking about the fear of not measuring up to the expectations we allow others to lay on us. The fear that we are not good enough. The fear that the job is bigger than our performance capability. The fear that we are letting others down by not being all they expect of us.

Probably there are no words that control human behavior more than, "What will others think?" We are intimidated by them time and again. Many of us never experience the dimensions of life or explore the potential of our capabilities because we are afraid. We are afraid that we are incompetent. We are afraid of ridicule or failure. We are afraid to take a chance.

In Nikos Kazantzakis' novel, the American friend of Zorba the Greek is reminded over and over of this adventurous life which has eluded him. He is both intrigued and threatened by Zorba's dances in the middle of the night. They lure him to leave the safe havens of prudence and custom in order to depart on great voyages to another world. Yet he is unable to respond. He sits there motionless and shivering. He is ashamed. He has felt this shame before whenever he caught himself not daring to do what supreme recklessness the essence of life called him to do. Yet never did he feel more ashamed than in the presence of Zorba.[2]

Many of us have felt that way. We sit before life, shivering, afraid to take a chance, for fear we will make fools of ourselves. We are afraid of what others will think. We are intimidated by life.

It is to us, therefore, that the good news speaks, "Fear not! For I who am life, I who brought you into being and cause to be what I cause to be, I who have given you your individuality and named you, I say you are mine, therefore, *live!*"

Karl Barth believed that when the Word of God addresses us, it gives us permission to live. The Word of God conveys life-giving power. The power in Isaiah's message is that God is in life as a hand is in a glove. Life, therefore, cannot destroy us. The good news is that we do not need to be afraid of life. Though it may have the appearance of the Enemy, it conceals, in reality, the God of grace. No matter how difficult it may seem, life cannot destroy us because life is the glove of God, our creator. We may encounter God as the adversary, but only because our humanity depends on it. Therefore, we can risk living. Life, rather than being destructive to our best interests, is a conspiracy of growth masterminded by the God of grace.

The psychologist might say that life is exposure to contradiction. Its deepest lessons are taught in the clumsiest of ways. To live is to incur guilt and regret. Human beings are creatures with potential, but this potential is found only in and through and despite the bumbling awkwardness of living. Children can mature into adulthood only by risking failure, accepting guilt, and gaining wisdom from their experience. We do not need to fear life. It conspires to make us grow. Fear not.

Paul, the theologian, put it more poetically when he said: "I am sure that neither death nor life, nor angels nor principalities, nor things present nor things to come, nor powers, nor height, nor depth nor anything else in this whole creation can ever separate me from Life—from the love of God."

Paul was saying, I can risk all these things because none of them can separate me from life, because life is of God. God has given me permission to live. In life and in death, in joy and in sorrow, with principalities of goodness and evil, I have been given permission to live.

This good news, however, is not simply a general permission. It is extremely specific. God is saying, "I who have called you, Jacob; I who have called you, Israel; I who have called you, William Robert McClelland; I tell you to live."

Consider, if you will, the miracle of my birth and, in the process, the miracle of your birth. At a point in time, one egg out of thousands of others in my mother ripened and would have died had it not been for the fact that within a period of twenty-four hours that egg was fertilized. But that particular egg survived. It did not die. It was fertilized by a sperm cell, one of over five hundred million other possibilities from my father's body. Most of its companions died in the process of trying to reach that egg, were killed by the acids in my mother's body, went in the wrong direction, or grew tired and gave up. Had any other sperm cell reached that egg, I would not have been. Somebody else would have been, but not me! It was a one-in-500-million long shot. But that particular cell made it. My conception took place.

Yet that is only half of the miracle. When that particular egg in my mother's body ripened, half of the 46 chromosomes in that egg were sloughed off. The half that remained and the half that were discarded were determined purely by chance. As if some kind of colossal bookmaker were setting the odds at one to eight million, the chromosomes happened to split the way they did. Had they split any other way, I would not be who I am. I would be different.

While this was happening in the egg cell of my

mother, the same process was taking place in that one sperm cell of my father. The chromosomes were splitting in another one in eight million chance. Again, if the split had taken place in any one of those millions of other ways, I would have been a different person. When you begin to calculate the odds of my being, they are astronomical.

Life has not only given me permission to live, it has given *me* an infinitely rare opportunity to live. There has not been another person like me in the history of the human race. There is no other person in the world like me, and there never will be another person like me. When I think of how close I came to not being here at all, I shudder. More to the point, I am humbled.

The astounding good news that Isaiah is proclaiming is that the God of grace, Yahweh, who causes to be what he causes to be, says, "Fear not. I, who was your one chance in the face of astronomical odds, created your uniqueness and gave it a name, I say, 'Live, William Robert McClelland.'"

I remember in grade school the embarrassment of recess. We chose up sides to play ball. I was not very good, and I stood there feeling afraid and inadequate. Intimidated and frightened, I wished that recess were over. Then I heard my name called. "Bob." How beautiful it sounded to me. Somebody wanted me on their team. And so I played. Poorly, but I played, because I had been called. My name had been sounded.

The gospel is the good news that life has sounded our name. We are called to life as Robert or Ralph, as Jane or Joyce, as Mary or Mark. We are called to live out the miracle of our uniqueness. Not to be copies of someone else. Not to try and be what other people think we should be, but to be fully ourselves.

The significance of being oneself is caught in these words by Lowell Streiker:

> Maturity or self-realization requires that I become aware of the unique, irreplaceable potentialities of my existence as a person and that I accept responsibility for actualizing them. Self-realization is a painful, gradual process marked by many reversals, defeats, and disappointments. Since what I was meant to be is different from what anyone else was meant to be, no formula, maxim, generalization, or dogma can distinguish for me between the real and the apparently real. Within all the circumstances which condition my existence, I must stumble along my path, discovering and actualizing the real "I."[3]

No excuses can cover up our failure to be ourselves. There is only one of you and one of me. If we blow it, no one else can do it for us. The story of Zusya makes the point. When getting old and nearing death, Zusya, the Rebbe of Annitol, said to his disciples, "After I die and go to the heavenly courts to be judged, God will not say to me, 'Zusya, why weren't you Moses?' Instead, He will say to me, 'Zusya, you could have at least been Zusya, so why weren't you?'"

A popular television commercial reminds us we only go around once. Life can be, and often is, painful, but we only have one crack at it. Nowhere in the Bible does

it say that we will be exempt from pain nor does it give
answers for the pain. But one thing the Bible does say:

> Fear not, I who created you, I who formed you,
>     I have called you by name, you are mine.
> When you pass through the waters, I will be with you;
>     and rivers, they shall not overwhelm you.
> When you walk through fire, you shall not be burned,
>     and flames shall not consume you. For I am Yahweh,
>         your God,
>     the Holy One of Israel, your Savior.
>
> (paraphrase)

# Epilogue

The grace of God comes in many ways to renew us and heal our brokenness. In these pages I have tried to share with you how his grace healed me when I was afraid to live and was embarrassed to die. Even though I could no longer speak with the tongues of other men or of angels, I found I was loved—loved by God and loved by people. I no longer felt like a cripple. That is the miracle to which I bear witness. I no longer needed a nice-sounding voice to feel whole. What follows, therefore, in no way adds to the miracle, but rather stands as a gift of grace in its own right.

Five years ago my attention was called to a newspaper article in which Illinois Congressman Tom Railsback was reported to have undergone a new surgical procedure for spastic dysphonia developed by Dr. Herbert Dedo of the University of California Medical Center. For all I knew, Dedo could have been some witch doctor, but the mention of University of California Medical Center made it sound credible. Still and all, I had been sent from pillar to post in search of a will- o'-the-wisp cure and so was not overly impressed by the newspaper account. The clipping gathered dust on my dresser for several weeks before I finally picked up the telephone and called Congressman Railsback. I was astounded at the ease with which he spoke. He told me of his surgery and what his voice had been like before it. As a result of our conversation, I made arrangements to go to San Francisco. It was, and is, Dr. Dedo's opinion that, in the majority of cases, spastic dysphonia is not psychosomatic, which is why counseling, though it certainly helps to restore a person's self-image, is ineffective in the restoration of the voice. The exact cause is still a mystery although a virus is suspected. In any case, he examined me and explained the nature of the surgery. It would mean severing the recurrent laryngeal nerve. This would allow one of the rigid vocal cords to relax thus enabling breath to flow around it more easily. Through speech therapy I would have to learn how to control the pitch and volume of my voice. My new voice, it was explained, would be lower in pitch and there would be some loss of volume. The doctor's enthusiasm was encouraging, however. I was convinced when he injected an anesthetic into the vocal cords and gave me a page of printed material to read. The tape recorder was turned on. I strangled through a sentence or two. The injection began to take effect. The words grew slippery. It was as if they were greased and came squirting out of my mouth. My eyes grew wide with amazement. Then addiction. It had been four and one-half years since I had spoken easily—normally. I had forgotten how effortlessly one can speak. I could not stop talking. I read all the words on the page and then began to recite everything I had ever committed to memory. Lincoln's Gettysburg address, Mark Anthony's eulogy from Julius Caesar, Hamlet's soliloquy, psalms from the Bible. It was a euphoric experience. The effect of the anesthetic lasted several hours. And then, as it wore off, the feeling of strangulation returned. I had made my decision, however. Surgery was scheduled for the next day.

Whatever else can be said about a hospital, it is a place where many people encounter God as the enemy. For some it is the place where serious illness is discovered or the news of it made known to family and patient. For others it is the place where the final *no* of God is uttered. For me it was a place of grace where, thanks to the miracle of medical science and the skill of Dr. Dedo, I underwent surgery and received in return a new voice. Like Job, I had met God as the enemy so that I might know him as the God of grace. And like Job, I received back what had been taken away—plus more. Not only did I have a new voice, but I had acquired a new appreciation of the miracle of being—both God's and my own.

In the days following my short stay in the hospital, I began the long, and at times frustrating, task of learning how to use and control my new voice. The work was made somewhat more bearable because I was enjoying the sights and sounds of San Francisco with my wife, not to mention the delightful adventure of exploring its cuisine. After some initial work with the speech therapist there, it was time to make the trip home and share my new voice with the Community of

Faith. I felt like a young schoolboy bringing a gift to his first date. I was nervous. I so wanted to present my voice to the members of the congregation at its best. They had suffered with me through the trauma of its loss and had loved and accepted me during those years when I strangled to share the Word with them. It had been "our" voice that I had taken to San Francisco, and now it was "our" voice that I was about to unveil in their midst. I wanted to present it to them as a gift—strong and beautiful.

It took nearly a year of speech therapy, but gradually my voice became strong and flexible. Now I am able both to laugh more easily and curse more loudly—both to the praise of God—for in many other ways he still encounters me as the Enemy in order that I may know him as the God of grace.

# Notes

**CHAPTER 1**

1. Edith Sommer Soderberg, *A Roomful of Roses*, rev. ed. (New York: Dramatists Play Service, [1954] 1956).

**CHAPTER 2**

1. Francis Thompson, "The Hound of Heaven" (Mt. Vernon, N.Y.: Peter Pauper Press), pp. 5, 18.
2. Paul Tillich, *The Shaking of the Foundations* (New York: Charles Scribner's Sons, 1948), pp. 161-62.

**CHAPTER 3**

1. Ibid., p. 42.
2. Thomas Kelly, *A Testament of Devotion* (New York: Harper & Row, 1941), p. 70.
3. Thornton Wilder, *The Eighth Day* (New York: Harper & Row, 1967), p. 135.

**CHAPTER 4**

1. John Dart, "Woody Allen, Theologian," *Christian Century*, 22 June 1977, p. 587.
2. Karl Barth, *The Epistle to the Romans*, 6th ed. (New York: Oxford University Press), p. 156.
3. Robert M. Brown, "On Learning from Crisis Situations," *Christianity and Crisis*, 30 September 1974, p. 213.
4. Elie Wiesel, *Messengers of God* (New York: Random House, 1976), p. 3.
5. Elie Wiesel, *Night* (New York: Avon Books, 1960), p. 10.
6. Dart, "Woody Allen," p. 587.

**CHAPTER 5**
1. Kelly, *A Testament of Devotion*, p. 56.
2. Karl Barth, *The Word of God and the Word of Man* (New York: Harper & Row, 1957), p. 84.

**CHAPTER 6**
1. Jack Slater, "Three Profiles in Courage," *Ebony Magazine*, March, 1973, p. 106.
2. Ibid., p. 101.

**CHAPTER 7**
1. Carl Jung, *Memories, Dreams and Reflections* (New York: Random House, Vantage Books, 1963), p. 91.
2. Claire Randall, "Theologians Choice," comp. Jane Day Cook, *A. D.*, April, 1974, p. 23.
3. Stephen J. Sansweet, "Life in a Commune Doesn't Have to Be Spartan and Dreary," *Wall Street Journal*, April, 1974.
4. Arthur Miller, *Death of a Salesman* (New York: International Creative Management, 1949).

**CHAPTER 8**
1. Archibald MacLeish, *J. B.* (Boston: Houghton Mifflin, 1961), pp. 144-45.
2. *Time Magazine*, 24 February 1975, p. 38.
3. Hannah Green, *I Never Promised You a Rose Garden* (New York: Hart, Rinehart and Winston, 1964), p. 24.

**CHAPTER 9**
1. Richard Rubenstein, *After Auschwitz* (Indianapolis: Bobbs-Merrill, 1966), p. 262.
2. Green, *I Never Promised You a Rose Garden*, p. 254.

**CHAPTER 11**
1. James Meredith, "Black Leaders and the Wish to Die," *Ebony Magazine*, May, 1973, p. 157.
2. Ibid., p. 158.
3. R. Lofton Hudson, "What One Easter Meant to Me," *The Christian Century*, 18 April 1973, p. 452.

**CHAPTER 12**
1. Elizabeth Kübler-Ross, "The Dying Patient as Teacher: An

NOTES FOR PAGES 134-152

    Experiment and an Experience," *Chicago Theological Seminary Register*, December 1966, p. 5.
2. Leo Tolstoy, "The Death of Ivan Illych," trans. Aylmer Mand, in *Ten Modern Short Novels*, ed. Leo Hamalian and Edmond L. Volpe (London: Oxford University Press, 1958), p. 34.
3. See Rudolf Bultmann, *Jesus Christ and Mythology* (London: SCM Press, 1958).

**CHAPTER 13**
1. Kurt J. Vonnegut, *Cat's Cradle* (New York: Dell Books, 1963), p. 149.
2. Nikos Kazantzakis, *Zorba the Greek*, trans. Carl Wildman (New York: Simon & Schuster, 1952).
3. Lowell D. Streiker, *The Promise of Buber* (J. B. Lippincott, 1969), pp. 13-14.